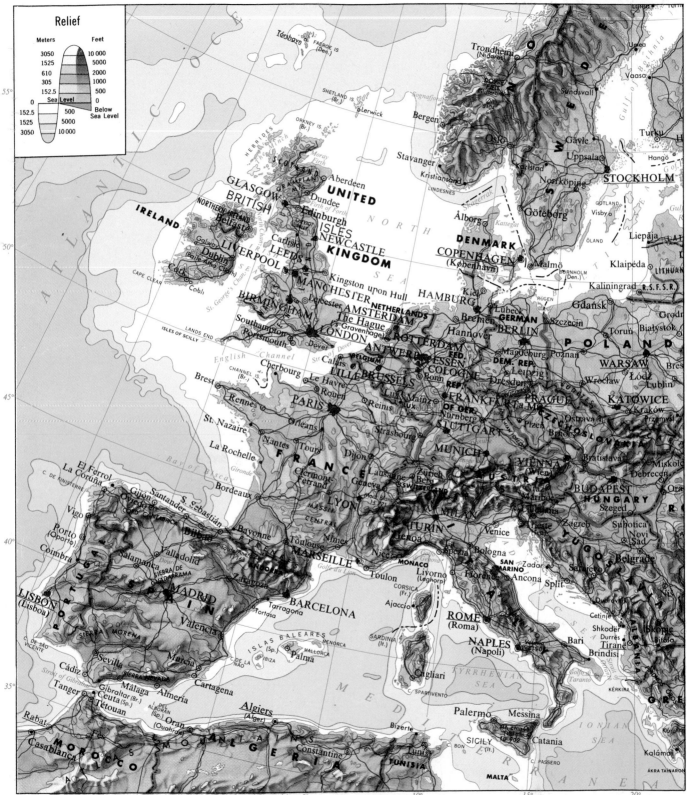

Relief

Meters		Feet
3050		10 000
1525		5000
610		2000
305		1000
152.5		500
0	Sea Level	0
152.5		500 Below
1525		5000 Sea Level
3050		10 000

5° Longitude West of Greenwich 0° Longitude East of Greenwich 5°

© Copyright by Rand McNally & Co., 84-S-18

Enchantment of the World

ITALY

By R. Conrad Stein

Consultants: Paul Giordano, Ph.D., Chairperson of Modern Foreign
Languages; Associate Professor of Italian, Rosary College, River Forest, Illinois

Dominic Candeloro, Ph.D., Fulbright Research Scholar in Italy, 1982-83;
Director of the 1979-81 Italians in Chicago Project (National Endowment for
the Humanities); Research Associate, Governor's State University, University
Park, Illinois

Consultant for Social Studies: Donald W. Nylin, Ph.D., Assistant Superinten-
dent for Instruction, Aurora West Public Schools, Aurora, Illinois

Consultant for Reading: Robert L. Hillerich, Ph.D., Bowling Green State
University, Bowling Green, Ohio

CP CHILDRENS PRESS ™
CHICAGO

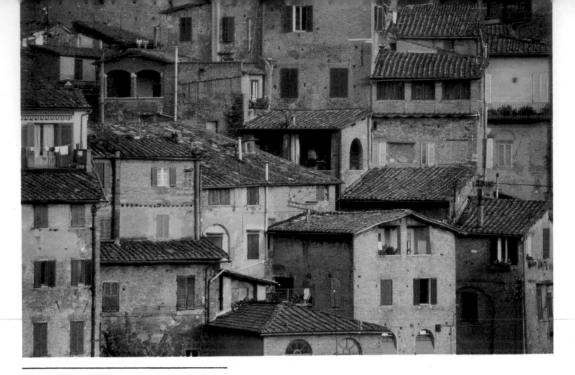

Homes in the medieval town of Siena

Library of Congress Cataloging in Publication Data

Stein, R. Conrad.
  Italy.

  (Enchantment of the world)
  Includes index.
  Summary: An introduction to the land, history, people, and culture of the southern European country that at one time ruled all of the western world.
    1. Italy—Juvenile literature. [1. Italy]
  I. Title. II. Series.
  DG417.S75 1984   945   84-11341
  ISBN 0-516-02768-9   AACR2

Picture Acknowledgments

Hillstrom Stock Photos: ©Carmen Trombetta: Cover, pages 5, 49 (left), 76 (bottom right); ©Paul J. Quirico: Pages 17, 99 (left); ©Milton and Joan Mann: Page 35; ©Lloyd Dinkins: Page 48 (left); ©Globe Photos: Pages 48 (right), 94; ©John J. White: Page 53; ©Michael Nelson: Page 86; ©Ephraim Kahn: Page 99 (right); ©Bob Zehring: Page 104
Nawrocki Stock Photo: ©William S. Nawrocki: Pages 4, 14 (left), 15, 76, (bottom left), 81, 84 (left), 85, 100 (bottom right), 106 (left)

Colour Library International: Pages 6, 9, 10, 14 (right), 18, 53 (bottom), 56, 87, 88 (top), 96, 98 (right), 105, 106 (right), 107, 109 (left), 111, 116
Jerry Reedy: Pages 8, 76 (top right)
Metropolitan Museum of Art: Gift of Nicolas Koutoulakis, 1955: Page 20 (left); Rogers Fund, 1903: Page 20 (right); Rogers Fund, 1912: Page 42; Bequest of Benjamin Altman, 1913: Page 45 (middle); Gift of J. Pierpont Morgan, 1917: Page 45 (left)
The Granger Collection: Pages 23, 28, 43 (left), 61
Picture Group: ©Daniel G. Dunn: Pages 25, 50; ©Lou Dematteis, Page 40;
Jerome Wyckoff: Pages 26, (top), 45 (right), 98 (left), 102
Worldwide Photo Specialty/Alexander M. Chabe: Pages 26 (bottom), 58 (top), 84 (right), 95, 100 (top and bottom left), 110
Joseph Antos: Pages 32, 33, 109 (right)
Historical Pictures Service, Chicago: Pages 43 (right), 66, 68, 90
Chandler Forman: Pages 49 (right), 58 (bottom), 64, 76 (top left), 79, 82, 88 (bottom)
UPI: Pages 70, 73 (left), 75
U.S. Army Photograph: Page 73 (right)
Wide World: Page 80
Root Resources: ©Kenneth Rapalee: Page 91
Len Meents: Map on page 39
Courtesy Flag Research Center, Winchester, Massachusetts 01890: Flag on back cover

Cover: Amalfi

Children of Salerno

TABLE OF CONTENTS

The Dolomites, a range of the Italian Alps

Chapter 1

THE LAND AND PEOPLE
OF ITALY

For more than two thousand years, poets have sung Italy's praises. "Hail, land of Saturn, sacred mother of earth's fruits," wrote Roman poet Virgil shortly before the birth of Christ. Nineteenth-century English poets echoed his words. Lord Byron called Italy "Mother of the arts. . .parent of our religion." Robert Browning wrote, "Open my heart and you will see/Graved inside of it, 'Italy.' "

Few countries have exerted so powerful an influence on the rest of the world. Once, Italy ruled all of the West. Centuries later, it led Europe into a brilliant new age called the Renaissance. No doubt timeless Italy still will be praised by poets two thousand years from now.

THE LAND OF ITALY

Italy is a long, narrow peninsula that juts into the Mediterranean Sea. On a map, it appears to be shaped like a boot, kicking Sicily as if that island were a soccer ball. At the knee of the boot and some 100 miles (161 kilometers) out to sea lies the island of Sardinia. Both Sicily and Sardinia are part of Italy.

A man rides his donkey along one of the steep, winding streets of Enna, Sicily.

The Italian peninsula is about 708 miles (1,139 kilometers) long and 130 miles (209 kilometers) wide at its widest point. Hills and mountains dominate the landscape. A topographical map shows a land that seems to have been twisted and squeezed by the hands of a giant. Italy's tallest mountains lie far to the north, where she shares a border with France, Switzerland, Austria, and Yugoslavia. There, in the Italian Alps, Monte Bianco (Mont Blanc) towers 15,771 feet (4,807 meters), making it the country's highest peak. Many mountains in the Italian Alps are snow covered the year round. Still, the winters are not unbearably cold, and the area is a favorite of skiers and other winter sports enthusiasts.

At the foot of the Italian Alps spreads the Po River valley. Unlike most of Italy, this fertile valley is very flat. It is watered every spring by melted snow flowing down from the Alps. Wheat, corn, and rice thrive there, making the valley Italy's "breadbasket."

South of the Po rises a range called the Apennines. These

The Sicilian town of Taormina has a breathtaking view of the Ionian Sea.

rugged mountains sweep like an arc around the Eternal City of Rome. Two thousand years ago the Apennines were covered by forests. But the ancients were as wasteful of natural resources as moderns are today. They cut down trees to provide mighty Rome with wooden warships. Rain washed away the topsoil and trees never grew again. Though forests can still be found in parts of the Apennines, many of the mountains stand stony and naked in the wind.

In fact, a good part of the Italian peninsula and the islands of Sardinia and Sicily are rocky and treeless. Still, the landscape offers breathtaking views of wind-polished rocks in majestic shapes. In the pure mountain air a traveler can struggle up a peak and behold a vista that will melt the heart.

Certainly the stony face of Italy has influenced the nation's architecture. Italian cities are constructed of stone that, like the mountains, seems to defy time. Many houses have original stone walls erected five hundred to a thousand years ago. Stone is everywhere in Italian villages and towns. Even Italian barns are made of solid stone.

Salerno is one of the dozens of towns and cities that dot the long coastline of Italy

Italian Riviera

Ligurian Sea

Adriatic Sea

Tyrrhenian Sea

Gulf of Naples

Isle of Capri

Mediterranean Sea

Ionian Sea

Italy's 2,685 miles (4,321 kilometers) of coastline are washed by five seas: the Ligurian and Tyrrhenian on the west, the Ionian and Mediterranean on the south, and the Adriatic on the east. For centuries, port cities such as Naples and Genoa have served as front doors to Italy. Today, the coastline serves as a magnet for tourists. Europeans of all classes flock to Italy's coasts in the spring. Along the Ligurian Sea, the Italian Riviera is particularly popular with northern Europeans. A visitor walking the beaches of the Italian Riviera hears nearly as much German as Italian. The island of Capri, nestled in the Gulf of Naples, was the vacation home for the Roman emperors Augustus and Tiberius some two thousand years ago. It remains a vacation retreat for tourists today.

CLIMATE

The country is often called "Sunny Italy." But clouds, rain, fog, and nagging cold can mar an Italian winter, particularly in the north. Northwestern coastal cities, however, are warmed by the waters of the Ligurian Sea, and winters there are more bearable.

Since Italy stretches almost directly north to south, its climate ranges from that of Europe to that of Africa. The Alps protect Italy from the extremes of a central European winter, but in January northern Italy can experience day after day of freezing weather. The southern end of the peninsula and Sicily have much warmer winters.

A chronic lack of rainfall plagues most of the nation. Only in the northern Po Valley can farmers depend on enough rainfall to grow crops. Dryness increases in the south. Much of the parched land in the southern half of the peninsula is suitable only for cattle grazing. In southern Sicily, less than 15 inches (38 centimeters) of rain falls each year.

THE PEOPLE

Italy is a crowded nation. In 1984 its population stood at about 58 million. Large tracts of land are barren and cannot support people in great numbers. For that reason, Italians crowd into cities or fertile regions. Italy has forty-four cities with populations of more than 100,000. Almost 60 percent of the Italian people live in cities or towns. The rich Po Valley comprises only 16 percent of the total landmass of Italy, yet 40 percent of the people live there.

Life in northern Italy is enormously different from life in the south. The north has rich farmland and is generally prosperous and industrialized. The south, however, has little industry and its farmland is of marginal value. Workers in the north earn twice as much as workers in the south. Although this is gradually changing, the disparity in wealth has existed for hundreds of years. For that reason, millions of southern Italians emigrated around the turn of this century. Most of today's Italian-Americans are from families that left the poorer southern half of Italy.

Italy is a nation of many regions. Until the late 1800s, the Italian peninsula was a patchwork of tiny kingdoms. They were created when rampaging tribes invaded Italy after the Fall of Rome in A.D. 476. From the north came the German-born Lombards, a tall, blond people who settled in a region still called Lombardy. They account for most of today's blond-haired, blue-eyed Italians. To the south, dark-skinned Arab people crossed the Mediterranean and settled in Sicily and the southern half of the peninsula. By 1100, those Arab Muslims had been conquered by the Normans. Later, French and Spanish people also settled in Italy.

These different groups carved out their own niches in the land, each shielded from its neighbors by rugged mountain chains. The tiny kingdoms grew into regions. Each region practiced its own customs, developed its own industries, and even spoke its own language. Only in recent years have Italians broken this pattern of regionalism. Until World War II, a person from the northern city of Milan considered a person from the southern city of Naples to be as foreign as an Englishman.

LANGUAGE

Regionalism dictated the development of the Italian language. At the time of the Roman Empire, Latin was the official language on the peninsula. When foreigners overran the Italian boot, a babble of tongues arose. The Italian language—an offshoot of Latin—began to emerge around the year A.D. 1000. But each region developed its own dialect of the new language. And people who speak different dialects often cannot understand one another.

Until the modern era, regional dialects split the Italian republic. In some instances, people living just a few miles from each other—but separated by a mountain range—had problems communicating.

Today, nearly all Italians use a standard dialect. Radio and television have helped to unify Italian-speaking people. Also, standard Italian is spoken and taught in all the nation's classrooms.

FAMILY LIFE

Large families used to be common in Italy. But inflation has sent the cost of food, housing, and education skyrocketing. So modern Italians, like most other Europeans, are having fewer children. A family unit often includes grandmothers, grandfathers, uncles, and aunts all living under the same roof. In the case of a poor family, all these people crowd into one house or apartment. No matter how poor its members may be, an Italian family shares everything it has.

Italians believe family problems take precedence over all other problems in life. The nation can go to war, the city can go bankrupt, the church can burn down. Over these tragedies an Italian will weep. But a death or severe illness in the family is a problem so desperate that it can destroy an Italian man or woman.

The Italian feels a sacred duty to protect and defend his family.

The cathedrals of San Rufino in Assisi (left) and Santa Maria del Fiore in Florence (right) are two of the thousands of Roman Catholic churches in Italy.

Rivalries often do exist between family members. But the family unit is bound together by the conviction that an injury to one is an injury to all.

RELIGION

Italy is 95 percent Roman Catholic. The Catholic church was based in Italy early in its history. The Holy See (the world headquarters of Catholicism) is located at Vatican City, a separate state lying in the center of Rome. In Vatican City is the office of the pope, who leads the world's 540 million Catholics.

The church is an important social and cultural institution. Italy has few family counselors or psychologists because most Italians take their problems to the local priest. In rural Italy, the church is

Schoolchildren in Verona on their way home

a source of lively entertainment. Church-sponsored parties are eagerly attended. Farm villages have patron saints, and once a year a feast is celebrated in that saint's honor. Some villages hold a dozen or more feasts during the course of a year.

EDUCATION

Italian law states that all children between the ages of six and fourteen must attend school. Since World War II, the government has enforced this law vigorously. It is a rare young Italian who cannot read or write.

Though the church is a powerful institution, Catholic schools are not numerous in Italy. About 90 percent of all elementary schoolchildren attend public schools, where priests teach religion.

At age fourteen, a student who elects to stay in school begins a

five-year program at a senior high school called a *liceo*.
A *liceo commerciale* trains students for careers in the business world. A *liceo scientifico* trains technicians and engineering students. The *liceo classico* is the traditional college-preparation school, but a graduate of any *liceo* may go on to college.

At the conclusion of their *liceo* courses, students face a rugged exam. The exam is sometimes called *maturitá*. Colleges are overcrowded and the tough exam weeds out below-average students.

Italy's colleges and universities are time-honored institutions. Half of them were founded before the year 1350. The University of Bologna was established near the end of the twelfth century.

The government is committed to maintaining an effective school system. In the 1950s, Italy spent 12 percent of her total national budget on education. By the 1970s, that figure had jumped to 25 percent.

POLITICS

If one word could describe the Italian character, it would be *individualistic*. Even though they have lived through periods of dictatorship, Italians still find it impossible to bottle up their ideas. Because of this intense desire for self-expression, Italians have led the Western world in music and the arts. But their powerful individualism has also weakened the government, which has had to bend to so many conflicting ideas.

Today Italy has at least fifteen major political parties. The Christian Democratic party is the country's largest. It has given Italian politics a much-needed sense of stability as the dominant power since World War II. Italy's Communist party, its second

A boy plays ball near the Communist party headquarters in a Venice courtyard.

largest, has more members than any other non-Communist country in Europe. While the Communists are not strong enough to dictate laws, they have the strength to influence voting in parliament. The third-largest group is the Socialist party.

The presence of so many political parties and so many diverse opinions makes it difficult for the government to make decisions. Individualism, the Italians' strength in art, is their thorn in government.

There is one subject, however, upon which all Italians agree. Their country has one of the richest histories of any nation in Europe, or, for that matter, the world. No one could argue: In Italy lies the heart and soul of Western culture.

This view of Rome from the Tiber River shows the Castel Sant' Angelo on the right and the dome of Saint Peter's Church in the background.

Chapter 2

IMPERIAL ROME

In 600 B.C., Rome was a simple farming village on the Tiber River in the middle of the Italian peninsula. Hundreds of similar villages dotted the countryside of Italy, North Africa, and Europe. Yet only one of those villages—Rome—became one of the greatest empires the world has ever seen. How Rome expanded is a story of courage and brutality, genius and savagery.

ROME IN ITS INFANCY

A legend asserts that Rome was founded by twin brothers abandoned on the bank of the Tiber. The babies, named Romulus and Remus, almost starved to death before a she-wolf nursed them to health. When they grew to manhood, the twins founded the city of Rome on the very spot where they had been left to die. It is said that Romulus traced the boundaries of Rome with his plow.

No physical evidence supporting the Romulus and Remus story has ever been found. Excavations do show that a people called the Latins began farming near the site of Rome as early as the 700s B.C. At the time, Italy was ruled by a mysterious people called the

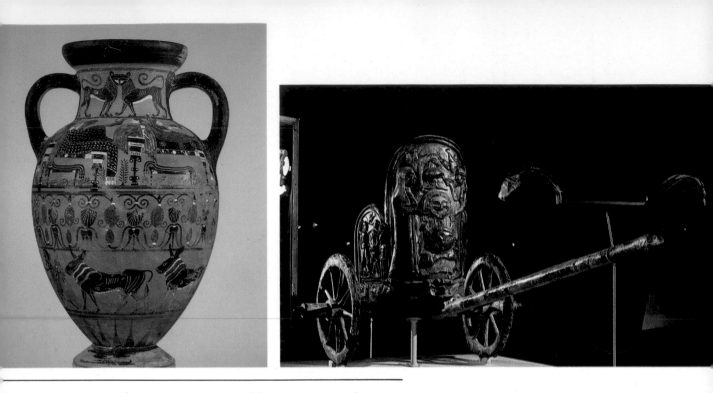

This terra-cotta vase and bronze ceremonial chariot were made by Etruscans between 575 and 540 B.C.

Etruscans. Evidence shows that the Etruscans were a highly civilized people who were fond of art and music. Etruscan kings ruled the village of Rome until 509 B.C. Then the Latins rebelled and drove them out. The Latins, later called the Romans, established a republic, a nation that has no monarch (king or queen).

THE GROWTH OF THE ROMAN REPUBLIC

Early Romans were farmers in a hostile land. The infant republic was surrounded by enemies. During the 400s B.C., Rome and a few friendly neighbors formed the Latin League for mutual protection. At the time, warfare in central Italy was almost constant.

Out of the ranks of simple farmers came a host of heroes who inspired later generations. The hero Horatius was said to have single-handedly fought off an entire Etruscan army while defending a key bridge. As a reward, the Roman government gave Horatius as much land as he could plow in one day. During an invasion in 458 B.C., Roman officials chose Cincinnatus to command the entire republic. They found him plowing a field on his small farm. Cincinnatus left his plow in mid-furrow, led the Roman army to victory, then returned to his field and calmly resumed plowing.

Largely because of the raw courage of her soldiers, Rome's territory grew. The early Romans showed little desire to forge an empire. They simply wanted to protect themselves. So they expanded their borders in order to neutralize their neighbors — and then their new neighbors, and so on. By 300 B.C., the Romans controlled almost the entire Italian peninsula.

While they expanded, the Romans introduced their language to other peoples. By the third century B.C., all of Italy spoke Latin. Romans soon carried Latin to every corner of Europe. For the first and only time in history, the educated people of Europe shared a universal tongue. Even today, Latin remains the official language of the Catholic church and is used and studied by scholars the world over.

THE PUNIC WARS

As the Roman republic's borders grew, her enemies became more far-flung. In 264 B.C. a dramatic series of three wars began between Rome and the state of Carthage, which lay on the northwest coast of Africa. The wars were called the Punic Wars. During one of them, Rome was nearly defeated by an outside invader for the first and only time in her early history.

The first Punic War, fought between 264 and 241 B.C., was conducted largely at sea. On land Roman soldiers were almost invincible, but her military had little experience with sea warfare. However, they outfitted each of their ships with a long bridge that had a spike jutting out of the far end. The bridges were attached to the ships by hinges and stood vertically. In battle, a Roman commander maneuvered his ship alongside an enemy vessel, then ordered the bridge to be pushed down. The bridge crashed into the enemy's deck, the spike dug in, locking the two vessels together, and Roman soldiers charged across. In that way, the Romans were able to use their superior ground troops at sea.

In the second Punic War, 218-201 B.C., the Romans faced an army led by one of the greatest military leaders of all time—the Carthaginian General Hannibal.

Hannibal led an army across the Strait of Gibraltar, through Spain and France, over the towering Alps, and attacked the Italian peninsula from the north. The march alone was an incredible achievement. Hannibal took some eighty thousand troops, twelve thousand horses, and squadrons of lumbering war elephants hundreds of miles into Italy. He won victories against the Roman army in unbelievably bloody battles at Lake Trasimeno in 217 B.C, and at Cannae in 216 B.C. For the next thirteen years, Hannibal remained in Italy, plundering the countryside. But he never was able to attack the city of Rome itself, nor was he able to break the tightly knit alliances Rome held with her neighboring cities. Finally, Rome counterattacked Carthage itself and Hannibal had to hurry back to North Africa to defend his homeland. He was eventually defeated in the Battle of Zama in 202 B.C.

The third and last Punic War, fought between 149 and 146 B.C., demonstrated the Roman thirst for vengeance and the severity of

On their way to attack Rome in the second Punic War, Carthaginian General Hannibal and his troops had to ferry their lumbering elephants over the Rhône River in France.

the punishment meted out to enemies. The Roman statesman Cato issued the famous demand *"Carthago delenda est."* ("Carthage must be destroyed.") And it was. Roman army commanders executed men and sold women and children into slavery. Carthaginian cities were razed and burned. Roman priests cursed the ruins. Finally, the ground was plowed and salt was strewn over it so that nothing could grow there for decades. Never again did once-powerful Carthage rise up against Rome.

After the Punic Wars, Rome's power spread into the eastern Mediterranean. At one time, the simple Roman farmers had stood in awe of the majesty of Greece. By 146 B.C., the Romans were the Greeks' masters.

While it seemed that Rome's expansion could not be checked by outside forces, the republic's real enemies lay within its own borders.

A CENTURY OF CIVIL WAR

From its beginnings as a republic, a struggle between rich and poor raged in Rome. The rich ruled the country through the Roman senate, while the poor fought for a larger voice in the government. The expansion of Roman territory magnified that struggle. Wealth flowing into the state from its many colonies made the rich richer, but did little to improve the life of the poor.

In 134 B.C., the poor found leadership in two brothers named Tiberius and Gaius Gracchus. They demanded that the huge old estates owned by the rich be broken up and the land redistributed to poor farmers. The Gracchus brothers reminded the senators that small farmers serving in the army had made Rome great. The senators, all of whom had large landholdings, responded by having both brothers killed.

The clash between poor classes and rich weakened the republic to the point where it eroded Rome's ancient alliances with neighboring cities. Wars flared up as cities declared themselves independent of Rome, and Rome had to send armies to suppress them.

Trying to bring order to the republic, two men set the stage for a power struggle filled with intrigue, love, hate, jealousy, and murder. The participants in the struggle were Pompey and Julius Caesar.

Julius Caesar, a great orator, politician, and writer, was perhaps the most brilliant general in Roman history. Armies under his command broadened Rome's power in France and the British Isles. But while Caesar fought at far-flung battlefronts, his rival Pompey took over Rome. When Caesar returned, civil war

Julius Caesar was an orator, politician, writer, and a brilliant general.

broke out as soldiers under his command battled soldiers under Pompey's command. Two centuries earlier, Romans fighting Romans would have been unimaginable. Finally, Pompey was stabbed to death by the brother of a beautiful, young Egyptian queen. Caesar later visited Egypt and fell in love with that queen. Her name was Cleopatra.

On the Ides of March (March 15), 44 B.C., Caesar walked on the grounds of the ancient Roman Forum where the senate debated. Suddenly he was pounced upon by members of the senate, and he, too, was stabbed to death.

Power then passed to both Caesar's grandnephew Octavian and

Emperor Augustus
built magnificent
buildings in the
Roman Forum.
In ruins for
centuries, this
forum was once
the center of
Roman government.

to Caesar's chief lieutenant Mark Antony. Mark Antony fell in love with Cleopatra, who was still brooding over the loss of Caesar. But Mark Antony had made a dangerous enemy in Octavian. In the Battle of Actium (31 B.C.) Mark Antony's forces were defeated by forces loyal to Octavian. In despair, Mark Antony, and later Cleopatra, committed suicide.

The Battle of Actium ended a century of revolution, but Rome would never be the same again. More than just a man had died when Caesar was killed. The republic died, too. For five hundred years, the proud Romans had boasted that their nation had no king or queen. But after Caesar's death, leaders of the nation wielded even more power—as *emperors* of mighty Rome.

ROME UNDER THE EMPERORS

After the death of the republic, some of the emperors promoted their own mad ambitions at a cost of great suffering to Rome and her neighbors. But other emperors used power wisely, to enhance the glory of Rome.

In 27 B.C., Octavian became Rome's first emperor. However, he was careful never to use that title. Instead he took the name Augustus, meaning "revered one." Augustus ruled Rome for forty-one years under a government so brilliant that it served less-able emperors for centuries to come. His wise rule healed the scars inflicted by a hundred years of civil war. He punished corrupt officials and lowered the taxes the colonies paid to Rome. The arts flourished under this regime, and many magnificient new buildings rose. He once boasted that he "found Rome brick and left it marble." Augustus died in A.D. 14. Many historians believe his rule—the Augustan Age—was the Golden Age of Rome.

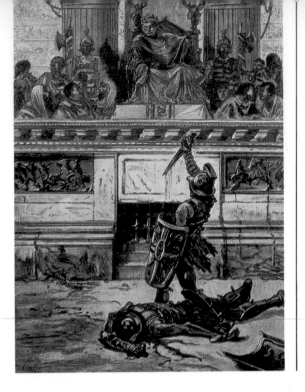

Nearsighted Emperor Nero often watched gladiators in the Roman arena through a corrective emerald eye lens.

No subsequent emperor won the confidence and love of the people as had Augustus. In the next hundred years, sixty-one different emperors presided over Rome. A few were outstanding, many were mediocre, some were inferior, and a few were insane.

The only long-lasting disservice Augustus did to the Roman people was to appoint Tiberius as his successor. Tiberius served for thirty-three years. He was a stern, selfish man, hated by the people.

From the point of view of history, the most significant event of Tiberius's reign occurred in the province of Judea. There a Roman governor named Pontius Pilate ordered the execution of a political prisoner—an execution that went unnoticed in Rome. The prisoner's name was Jesus.

In the year A.D. 54, a sixteen-year-old boy named Nero became emperor. In his first year of office, Nero poisoned his adopted brother. Next he made three unsuccessful attempts to kill his mother. Finally, Nero accused her of plotting against the empire and had her executed.

Nero claimed talents as a poet and singer. To make certain he had an audience, the emperor ordered members of his court to his private theater. According to one Roman writer, "While he [Nero] was singing, no one was allowed to leave the theater even for the most urgent reasons. And it was said that some women gave birth to their children there."

A great fire destroyed Rome in the year A.D. 64. Many Romans believed that Nero had ordered the fire because he had grandiose plans to rebuild the city. Some authors claimed that Nero played his lyre while the fire raged. A defiant Nero accused Christians of setting the fire. Christianity was a new, but growing, religious sect. Nero ordered hundreds of Christians put to death in the Roman arena.

Nero committed suicide in the year 68. It is said that his last words were, "What an artist the world is losing." But even under a madman, the machinery of government, so well established by Augustus, kept the empire together.

Many Roman emperors were superb leaders. Prosperity reached its height during the reign of what historians call the "five good emperors." Those five—Nerva, Trajan, Hadrian, Antonius Pius, and Marcus Aurelius—served in turn from the years A.D. 96 to 180. Each was honest, brave, and devoted to his duty. Under Trajan (98-117), the borders of the Roman Empire swelled to their greatest expanse—from North Africa to England, and from Egypt to the Black Sea. In all, the empire covered some 2.5 million square miles (about 6.5 million kilometers).

At that time, Rome was so powerful that she had no major enemies. Other than frontier flare-ups, Rome fought no wars for two hundred years. No other society before or since has been able to maintain peace for such a long time. Historians call that remarkable period the *pax Romana* ("Roman peace"). Because there were no wars to waste resources, Rome's standard of living rose dramatically.

However, even at the height of Rome's glory, trouble began brewing on her eastern and western frontiers. Barbarian tribes were growing in numbers and might. They longed to push back the borders of Rome. At first, few Romans worried about those backward people who wanted to challenge their mighty empire. But historian Cassius Dio, who lived during the height of Rome's power, must have caught a mysterious glimpse into the future. He wrote, "Our history now plunges from a kingdom of gold to one of iron and dust."

THE END OF GREATNESS

After the reign of the five good emperors, there began a three-hundred-year period that historians call Rome's "decline and fall." The steady weakening and eventual collapse of the empire were caused both by wars along its borders and by strife within them.

Marauding barbarian tribes to the east and west forced Rome to triple the size of her army. This sent taxes skyrocketing. The standard of living collapsed. Service in the army took so many men that foreign workers had to be employed to run the farms and mills. For ages, foreigners had drifted into Rome looking for work. Many were granted Roman citizenship even though their loyalties lay with their homelands.

The greatly expanded army began taking over Roman politics. During one sixty-seven-year period, the army pushed twenty-nine emperors and claimants on and off the throne. One of the so-called barracks emperors was a Thracian named Maximinius who spoke hardly any Latin and had never seen the city of Rome.

Jealousies among army commanders led to civil wars. At the same time, the barbarian tribes nibbled away at Rome's borders.

Even in the declining years, however, Rome found two outstanding emperors. Diocletian took power in 284, and with great energy and drive stopped the civil wars. He also divided the empire into eastern and western parts because he believed the territory was too vast to be governed by one man.

Another outstanding leader in Rome's later years was Constantine I, who ruled from 306 to 337. He built the city called Constantinople, which became the capital of the Eastern Roman Empire. Constantine claimed to have seen a miraculous cross in the sky one morning before a battle in which he defeated his enemies. Because the cross was the sacred symbol of the Christian religion, Constantine then legalized Christianity in Rome. The centuries of Roman persecution of Christians finally ended. On his deathbed, Constantine was baptized a Christian.

But even those two capable emperors could not halt the downward spiral of Rome. In 401, the barbarian Visigoths swept across the Alps into northern Italy. Nine years later, they burst through the walls of Rome itself—the first foreign invaders ever to enter the Eternal City. The Visigoths were followed by other barbarian tribes who marched across the Italian peninsula and over the vast territories that once had been the proud and invincible empire of Rome.

As a republic and empire, Rome's career spanned a thousand years. Her achievements were many. Still, contradictions abound in her history. Modern students of Rome are awestruck by her accomplishments, but appalled by her excesses.

The Pantheon in Rome, originally built as a temple to all the gods, has a front porch built in the traditional style of Greek temples, illustrating the extent to which Roman architects borrowed from the masterful Greeks.

ARTS AND ARMIES

In art, literature, architecture, and religion, Romans were borrowers rather than originators. Of all the cultures they encountered, they borrowed most avidly from the masterful Greeks. As the Roman poet Horace put it, "Captive Greece took Rome captive." Roman buildings bear a strong resemblance to Greek architecture. Many of the Roman gods were copies of earlier Greek gods; the Romans merely gave them Latin names. The Romans were immensely practical people. They believe that if they could not improve the high culture achieved by the Greeks, then at least they should borrow from the best.

The Romans did display an original genius in the art of warfare. Their war machines, designed with astonishing cleverness, included huge wheeled catapults that could lob heavy boulders great distances.

Still, wars are ultimately won by men, not devices. The Romans brought to the field courageous troops commanded by intelligent officers. Youths from wealthy families began to study battle tactics

The Appian Way, one of ancient Rome's marvelous roads

in school at the age of nine or ten. The upper classes produced many brilliant Roman generals, including Caesar and Pompey. The poor were expected to serve in the army, obey orders, and give their lives without question. A combination of superior officers, fearless troops, and brilliantly conceived equipment fielded an army that conquered the world.

Fighting battles was not the army's only function. "All roads lead to Rome," says a proverb. The marvelous roads that crisscrossed the empire were built largely by the army. They were not dusty, muddy paths. Roman roads were packed hard by thousands of workers, then covered with flat paving stones. They even had drainage ditches and sewers. In all, some 50,000 miles (80,467 kilometers) of roads connected all corners of the empire. The roads were built so well that many remain in use today.

BREAD AND CIRCUSES

To the ancient Romans, the bloody and brutal events that took place in the huge Colosseum were called "the games." Gladiator contests were as popular as soccer games are in Europe today. The Roman historian Suetonius wrote, "Such a throng flocked to these shows that...the press was often such that many were crushed to death." Most gladiators were slaves or prisoners of war. They had to begin their contests by saluting the emperor's box and chanting, "Hail, Emperor. We who are about to die salute you." A superb gladiator could become a popular hero and eventually win his freedom. However, mediocre fighters died in the sand when the emperor and the crowd signaled "thumbs down," meaning "show no mercy."

The bloodthirsty crowd seemed to enjoy unusual acts most of all. Gladiators were often pitted against wild beasts. A male dwarf might fight a woman to the death. Christians or condemned criminals were thrown into the arena among lions that had been starved. During these events, vendors sold rolls and sausages in the stands.

Many Roman intellectuals were appalled by the brutality and the carnage of the games. But the government believed that the common people loved and demanded such entertainment. Even during prosperous eras, unemployment was high in Rome. The government was always wary of the thousands of jobless men who wandered the streets. So it provided the people with free grain to make bread and free entertainment in the Colosseum. Meanwhile, the intellectuals lamented that all the masses really wanted were "bread and circuses."

ROMAN LAW AND LEGACY

"What sort of thing is civil law?" asked Roman statesman Cicero. "It is of a sort that cannot be bent by influence, or broken

The huge Roman Colosseum was the scene of bloody and brutal spectacles in which
gladiators were forced to fight each other, often to the death, or were
pitted against wild beasts, including lions, tigers, crocodiles, and elephants.

by power, or spoiled by money." More than any other ancient people, the Romans revered the law. As a rule, free Roman citizens were safer from unfair persecution by their government than any other people in the ancient world.

Roman law dates back to twelve tables written by republican officials in the year 450 B.C. Those early laws guaranteed Roman citizens certain rights. Over the thousand years of Roman history those rights expanded. In A.D. 527, Eastern Emperor Justinian drew up a new table of laws based on Roman law. The tone of those laws is astonishingly modern.

No one suffers a penalty for what he thinks. No one may forcibly be removed from his house. A father is not a competent witness for a son, nor a son for a father. In inflicting penalties, the age and inexperience of the guilty party must be taken into account.

The Roman system of law was so complete and so readily adaptable that many countries later based their legal systems on Roman ideas. Roman law influenced the writing of the American Constitution—a document that has governed the United States for more than two hundred years.

In the year 476, Romulus Augustulus, the last emperor of the Western Roman Empire, was deposed by Odoacer, a German tribal chief. The Eastern Empire remained, with its capital at Constantinople. But Rome of old—Italian Rome—would never rise again.

However, Roman institutions continue to affect the life and culture of lands the ancients never dreamed of. Because of Rome's thousand-year impact on history, the world will always be a different place. Rome never really died, and it never will.

Chapter 3

THE NEW LIGHT OF ITALY

The Fall of Rome left the Italian peninsula open to invasion by barbarian tribes. The Visigoths, Ostrogoths, Vandals, and finally the Lombards all swept into Italy. Though many soon left, some stayed to carve out their own territories. Italy became a patchwork of small countries and even smaller city-states. She remained a divided nation for the next thirteen centuries.

THE HOLY ROMAN EMPIRE

Politically, Italy was divided roughly into thirds. The Lombards established strong kingdoms in the north. The pope, head of the now-powerful Catholic church, presided over the Papal States, a territory in the middle of the peninsula. Southern Italy and Sicily were claimed by various tribes until the founding of a country called the Kingdom of the Two Sicilies.

In 962, King Otto I of Germany and the pope established the Holy Roman Empire in an attempt to unite Italy with Germany. The pope hoped the newly converted German tribes would protect the church from non-Christian invaders.

The territory claimed by the Holy Roman Empire included all of present-day northern Italy, Switzerland, and Germany. But the empire had little power over the vast lands it claimed; it was an empire in title only. French author Voltaire described it as "neither holy, nor Roman, nor an Empire." Still, various German kings claimed the empty crown of the Holy Roman Empire until the year 1806.

ITALY DURING THE MIDDLE AGES

The Middle Ages is the period between the Fall of Rome in 476 and the emergence of the modern world in the 1500s. The era can be thought of as a bridge connecting old and new Europe. The Middle Ages began with a decline in culture, but ended with an intellectual awakening called the Renaissance.

The immediate results of the Fall of Rome were disastrous for Italy. Law and order broke down. Art and literature suffered because few people had the time or money for those pursuits. The intellectual world became dominated by the Catholic church, which discouraged scientific inquiry. The scientific knowledge of the Greeks was forgotten. Latin died out as a spoken language, though it persisted until the seventeenth century as a written language. A new language similar to modern Italian developed in the peninsula's many regions.

At the beginning of the Middle Ages, travel and foreign trade dwindled. Weeds sprouted from cracks in the marvelous roads built by the Roman army. Men and women lived their entire lives without venturing out of the villages in which they had been born. In the city of Rome, the once-stunning buildings and statues crumbled. Wolves howled on the city's outskirts. Fear and superstition dominated the lives of the people.

By the year 1000 small Italian city-states began to rise to positions of great importance. Their development brought great changes to the land. In the north, Florence, Venice, Genoa, Bologna, Milan, and Pisa became centers of manufacturing and trade.

In the south, Palermo and Naples developed into important artistic capitals. Seaport cities, such as Amalfi on the Gulf of Salerno, built and operated huge fleets of ships. These maritime centers reestablished the lively trade that had flourished during the time of Rome. During the 1100s and 1200s, Italian ships took armies of Christian Crusaders from Europe to the Holy Land, which they hoped to recover from the Muslims. Merchants in the city-state of Venice grew rich supplying the Crusaders.

The twelfth-century Norman cathedral in Palermo contains the tomb of Holy Roman Emperor Frederick II.

The rise of the city-states stimulated intellectual life on the Italian peninsula. People exchanged ideas and began thinking beyond the narrow channels allowed by the church. One of the emerging intellectuals was Frederick II (1194-1250), a German whose father had conquered southern Italy and Sicily. As a Holy Roman emperor, Frederick II was one of the most brilliant rulers of the Middle Ages. In addition, he excelled as a soldier, scientist and poet. He encouraged sculptors, artists, and architects to come to his capital at Palermo and beautify that city. Frederick II also established major universities at Salerno and Naples.

Frederick II was a forerunner of the men who would soon lead Italy into a dazzling new era. He was knowledgeable in many fields—the arts, literature, science, medicine, and history. In the late 1200s and early 1300s, Italians with a broad range of talents propelled Europe into a golden age called the Renaissance.

THE RENAISSANCE

The French word *Renaissance* ("rebirth") describes the cultural awakening that occurred in Europe roughly between the years 1300 and 1600. Scholars rediscovered the knowledge once possessed by the Greeks and Romans. The focus of art, literature, and philosophy shifted from the heavens toward the world of human beings.

Humanism is a way of looking at the world which emphasizes the role of human beings. This belief in the importance of human activities, held sacred by the Romans, was rekindled during the Renaissance. The church-dominated belief was that God, not man, should be the center of interest. The church of the Middle Ages urged people to reject this world and conduct their lives in preparation for the next.

Despite their conflict with the church, most Renaissance thinkers were deeply religious. God remained the Almighty Supreme Being, but the stature of men rose to become almost godlike. Renaissance humanists believed that man was God's most cherished creation. God, therefore, approved of man finding glory in his own world and in his own acts.

The Renaissance was a period of curiosity and adventure. Renaissance thinkers probed the wonders of science and the arts. Painters and sculptors attempted bold new methods. Sailors ventured into unknown waters. Scientists performed daring experiments in physics, astronomy, and medicine. But above all, Renaissance thinkers studied man himself.

Wealthy Renaissance families filled their libraries with beautifully illuminated manuscripts. This detail of an illuminated letter S is from a fifteenth-century Italian manuscript.

TRADE AND BANKING

Without wealthy families there would have been no Renaissance. The wealthy had the leisure time to read and to admire art. As one prominent citizen of northern Italy wrote, "What can be more desirable to a well-regulated mind than the enjoyment of leisure with dignity?"

Despite the poverty of most of Italy, northern city-states such as Florence, Venice, and Milan produced a few very wealthy families. Their wealth was based on either banking or foreign trade.

Both Christopher Columbus (left) and Marco Polo (shown at right departing Venice for the East) were superb Italian sailors and fearless explorers.

Italians had long distinguished themselves as superb sailors and fearless explorers. In the late 1200s, Venetian trader Marco Polo boldly traveled into the heart of remote China. Some two hundred years later, another Italian, Christopher Columbus, read the lively stories Marco Polo had written about his travels. With a commission from the king and queen of Spain, Columbus sailed westward in the hope of arriving at the mysterious East. Instead, he discovered the American continent.

Both Marco Polo and Columbus ventured into unknown territory in search of trade. Silk from China and spices from India fetched high prices in Italy and other parts of Europe.

However, it cost dearly to outfit a ship or pay for an overland camel caravan to bring goods from the Orient. To obtain money, traders turned to bankers. Italians became the world's most skilled bankers. In pre-Renaissance Italy banking was conducted from benches set up near the market.

THE RICH AND POOR IN RENAISSANCE ITALY

During the Renaissance, wealthy Italian families lived in palatial houses, ate elegant meals, and were attended by dozens of servants. But few rich men were idle. They tended to the daily demands of their businesses. Most also held at least one office in local government. The rich were expected to give money to struggling artists and writers. Sponsoring a talented artist enhanced a family's prestige and political power. It also served as a great impetus to creative work.

Many wealthy families lived in the northern Italian city-state of Florence. The most important of these were the famous Medicis, who made their fortune in banking. From the 1400s to the 1700s, the Medici family supported the arts and ruled Florence almost continuously. The Medicis maintained a library of more than eight hundred books. At the time, most books were handwritten and very expensive. Still, the Medici library was open to students and teachers without charge.

The most famous member of the family was Lorenzo de' Medici, also called Lorenzo the Magnificent. He supported countless artists, scholars, and poets. From 1469 to 1492, Lorenzo ran the government of Florence. Under Lorenzo and his family's direction, Florence became an elegant city of museums, libraries, schools, statues, and fountains. However, many citizens complained that Lorenzo's lavish spending on the arts was bankrupting their city.

While the rich lived in luxury, the Italian poor struggled to exist. Florence was perhaps Italy's wealthiest city, yet in 1457 some thirty thousand families—nearly one third of the population—were listed on government records as being paupers.

These exquisite pendants of gold, enamel, and jewels were created by Renaissance craftsmen for wealthy Italian families.

The Medici Chapel in Florence

Beggars, including half-starved children, were common sights.

In the country, the poor worked on land leased from large landowners. Tenant farmers had to give a percentage of their crops to the landowners. Often this rent payment was so high that farm families had little to eat during the long winter. Revolts by the poor were brutally put down by soldiers hired by the landowners.

The children of the poor rarely had a chance to develop whatever talents they might have had. Poor children never saw the inside of a classroom or learned to read and write. Consequently, most of the great artists, writers, and scientists of the Renaissance came from the upper or middle classes.

THE BLACK DEATH

In the year 1348, a Russian ship moored in Genoa, Italy carried a dreaded disease that today is called bubonic plague. At that time it was known as the Black Death because the victims' skin broke out in black spots before they died. The disease was spread by fleas that lived in the fur of rats. Infected rats from that ship carried their deadly fleas to rats living in the streets of Genoa. A disastrous epidemic then struck northern Italy and, like fire, swept over all of Europe.

One Italian who survived the Black Death gave this chilling account of the terror:

"Neither relatives nor friends, nor priests accompanied the corpses to the grave. . . .In many places in the city trenches were dug, very broad and deep, and into these the bodies were thrown, and covered with a little earth; and thus layer after layer until the trench was full; and then another trench was begun. And I, Agniolo di Tura. . .with my own hands buried five of my children in a single trench, and many others did the like. . . .And no bells rang and nobody wept no matter what his loss, because almost everyone expected death. . . .And people said and believed, 'This is the end of the world.' "

In one year a third of the population of Italy is said to have died from the Black Death. Death in such staggering proportions had strange effects on people's minds. Poor people refused to work. City markets closed. Farmers' fields turned to weeds. The once lively Italian cities became hushed, ghostly places populated by dazed people who moved like sleepwalkers. Survivors were haunted by nightmares for the rest of their lives.

The dreadful disease killed one of every four persons on the

European continent. Recurring episodes of the plague ravaged Europe for centuries afterward. But despite these horrors, the light of Renaissance art and thought continued to burn brightly in Italy.

RENAISSANCE PAINTING AND SCULPTURE

To a viewer, paintings done by artists up to the early Middle Ages appear to be flat. There is no difference between the background and the foreground, no feeling of depth. Renaissance artists gave their canvases a natural, almost three-dimensional feeling. That sense of depth is what artists today call perspective.

The first major artist to experiment with perspective was the Italian, Giotto (1267?-1337). Though many historians consider him to be pre-Renaissance, Giotto's paintings had a powerful influence on the Renaissance masters who followed him. He boldly made the background objects in his paintings smaller and more faded than the foreground objects. The results were natural-looking scenes in which distant objects were seen as having less detail than closer objects. Giotto's most famous works are a series of wall paintings, or frescoes, in a chapel in the city of Padua.

Developing the principles of perspective even further was Italian artist Tommaso Guidi Masaccio (1401-1428). Masaccio created solid-looking forms on his canvas by skillful use of light and shade. His most important works are the frescoes on the walls of the church of Santa Maria del Carmine in Florence.

The 1500s are often called the period of the High Renaissance. Artists by then had completely mastered the techniques of perspective. Painting exploded like a flower in full bloom.

Leonardo da Vinci (1452-1519) was not only a skilled painter

The Leonardo da Vinci memorial in Milan (left) honors one of the greatest painters of the Italian Renaissance. His painting The Savior *is shown on the right.*

but also an inventor, a scientist, an architect, a city planner, and a student of astronomy, botany, and medicine. What is perhaps the most famous painting in the world was completed in 1504 by Leonardo. The curious smile on the face of his *Mona Lisa* has fascinated viewers for nearly five centuries.

Leonardo kept notebooks containing drawings of his inventions. Many of those notebooks survive and are studied by scholars today. He had a strange fascination for war machines. His drawings show guns, battering rams, siege equipment, slings, and catapults. He also sketched and described what he called "covered chariots" behind which foot soldiers could safely advance. Clearly, he had the modern battle tank in mind. He even

Michelangelo carved the Pietà *(left) when he was only twenty-three. Five years later he painted the* The Holy Family *(right), which hangs in the Uffizi Gallery in Florence.*

made a design for a flying machine and a parachute. Because Leonardo wrote his notes backwards, they have to be read with the aid of a mirror.

Another leading painter of the High Renaissance was Michelangelo (1475-1564). No one in history combined such power in sculpting, painting, architecture, and poetry as did Michelangelo. He delighted in working on grandiose projects—the bigger the better. He loved the challenge of daring, larger-than-life works.

At the age of twenty-three, Michelangelo carved his magnificent statue called the *Pietà*. The marble statue shows Mary cradling Jesus after the Crucifixion. It now stands in Saint Peter's Church

About the difficult conditions under which he had to work while painting the ceiling of the Sistine Chapel (left), Michelangelo wrote a humorous poem containing these lines: "My beard turns up to heaven, my nape falls in fixed on my spine; my breast-bone visibly grows like a harp; a rich embroidery bedews my face from brush-drops thick and thin."

in Rome. Also in Rome is the Sistine Chapel for which Pope Julius II commissioned Michelangelo to paint Biblical scenes across the ceiling. For four years, Michelangelo lay flat on his back on a scaffold, painting brilliant pictures that include God creating man.

Raphael (1483-1520) is especially famous for his many striking Madonna and Child paintings.

Renaissance sculpture also shattered the traditions of the Middle Ages, when figures were carved with long, flowing robes. Italian Renaissance sculptors undressed their models, preferring to show the naked human figure. One splendid sculptor of the Italian Renaissance was Donatello (1386-1466). His marvelous work *David* was the first large statue cast in bronze since the time of the Romans.

RENAISSANCE ARCHITECTURE

Among the most stunning gifts Renaissance masters bequeathed to future generations are the breathtaking churches, buildings, fountains, and plazas that grace Italian cities. Two major influences can be seen in Renaissance structures: a reverence for the classical style of old Rome and the prevailing humanistic philosophy of the times.

The most influential architect during the early Renaissance was Filippo Brunelleschi of Florence (1377?-1446). In 1420 he began work on the dome of the Cathedral of Florence. The project took sixteen years. Like many other Renaissance architects, Brunelleschi designed his buildings and supervised their construction. He devised ingenious methods for raising huge beams up to dizzying heights. When the dome was completed, architects from all over Europe came to gaze in amazement at this marvelous structure. Brunelleschi also designed the splendid Pazzi Chapel in Florence. The chapel is bedecked with Corinthian columns like those used in buildings of old Rome. Another major Renaissance architect was Leon Battista Alberti (1404-1472). Also a scholar, a painter, and an author, Alberti devoted much of his youth to the study of Greek and Roman culture. In the mid-1440s, he published a series called *Ten Books on Architecture*. The works contained ideas on reviving classical Roman architecture, and on the need for building structures in a humanistic manner.

The term *Renaissance man* is often used to describe an especially gifted person of many talents. Many Renaissance figures were both artists and architects—and perhaps scientists and poets, as well. Michelangelo, for example, was not only a marvelous painter and sculptor, but also a gifted architect. During the late Renaissance, he contributed to the most grandiose construction project of his era when he designed the great ribbed dome of Saint Peter's Church in Rome.

Renaissance architects delighted in working on projects that were grand in scale. City planning—the process of guiding the development of cities and towns—appealed to them. They replaced the crowded and airless look of medieval towns with open plazas in which stood statues and fountains. Superb examples of this humanistic trend in city planning include the plaza in front of the Cathedral of Saint Mark in Venice and the broad plaza of Saint Peter's Church in Rome.

The cities of Florence, Venice, Milan, and Pisa hold the most-famous examples of Renaissance buildings. But Italy has a way of surprising a visitor. Tucked away in a mountain village one can stumble on a magnificent five-hundred-year-old-church that somehow has been overlooked by the writers of guidebooks. Throughout Italy, hundreds of buildings stand as silent monuments to the genius of Renaissance architects.

RENAISSANCE LITERATURE

Up to the early 1400s, Italian scholars wrote in Latin, as if the Italian language were too lowly a tongue for the written word. But the sweeping humanistic ideas of the Renaissance changed this notion. The first major writer bold enough to write in Italian was

The plazas in front of the Cathedral of Saint Mark in Venice (above) and Saint Peter's Church in Rome (below) are superb examples of Renaissance humanistic city planning.

poet Dante Alighieri (1265-1321). His greatest work was the long poem called *The Divine Comedy.* Dante himself is the major character in the poem, and the story takes him on a moving journey from hell to purgatory to paradise. Dante was not a purely Renaissance writer. In both structure and content, *The Divine Comedy* is a medieval poem. But Dante's work had a profound influence on the Renaissance writers who followed.

The poet Petrarch (1304-1374) is considered by many historians to be the father of humanism. His poetry revered people, not the saints or heavenly figures about whom previous poets had written. Petrarch was a frequent traveler from city to city in Renaissance Italy. About his constant wanderings, he wrote these melancholy lines:

> No land, now, no air is constant for me;
> As I am nowhere a dweller, so am I a pilgrim everywhere.

Giovanni Boccaccio (1313-1375) greatly admired both Dante and Petrarch. His most famous book, *The Decameron,* tells of a group of young men and women who flee Florence to escape the Black Death. Once settled in the country, they pass their time by telling stories. One hundred different stories are told in *The Decameron,* giving a fasinating view of Italian society of the time.

Poet Ludovico Ariosto (1474-1533) was a true Renaissance spirit. He loved the beauty of fields, streams, and mountains. As painters try to capture beauty on canvas, Ariosto tried to bring natural beauty to his written lines. His masterpiece, a long poem called *Orlando Furioso,* tells of a group of knights who travel the world defending helpless people and seeking adventure. Ariosto's robust sense of humor dominates nearly all of his work.

The most important political thinker of the Renaissance was Niccolo Machiavelli (1469-1527). He is often thought of as the father of modern political science. His famous book *The Prince* tells leaders how to gain and keep political power. Machiavelli advised them to use any means necessary—including cruelty and deception—to maintain political order. To this day, a politician who stays in office through underhanded means is said to be acting in a Machiavellian manner. Actually, Machiavelli condoned foul play only as a last resort to prevent the breakdown of the state.

Torquato Tasso, one of the great poets of the late Renaissance, was born in Sorrento in 1544. Romantic love fills many of his poems.

Michelangelo's many talents included poetry. He often used poetry to speak out against the evil he saw around him.

SCIENCE AND MEDICINE

Among the most courageous men of the Renaissance were the scientists, who sometimes came to the shocking conclusion that the revered Greeks were wrong. Galileo (1564-1642) is an outstanding example of such an Italian Renaissance scientist.

Often called the founder of experimental science, Galileo believed that repeated experiments could prove or disprove scientific principles. The Greek philosopher Aristotle had stated that heavy objects fell faster than light objects. Galileo disagreed. He believed that gravity pulled all objects toward the earth with the same force. Certainly a feather falls more slowly than a rock, but this, thought Galileo, was due to air resistance. According to a famous story, he climbed to the top of the Leaning Tower in the

To test his theory of falling bodies, it is said that Galileo dropped two rocks of unequal weight from the Leaning Tower of Pisa (shown here next to the cathedral).

Italian city of Pisa and dropped two rocks of unequal weight. Both rocks struck the earth at the same time. After repeating the experiment many times, Galileo established the principle held today that all falling bodies fall at the same speed.

Galileo was also an astronomer. To aid his work, he made telescopes that were larger and more powerful than any others in use at the time. His studies in astronomy brought Galileo into a confrontation with the Catholic church. Galileo agreed with the theory advanced by Polish astronomer Copernicus that the earth moves around the sun. The church bitterly opposed this theory. Because of his beliefs, Galileo was put on trial and sentenced to a prison term. He never actually went to prison, however, but was confined instead to his home in Florence.

By the sixteenth century, Italy led all of Europe in medical research. One center for this research was the University of Padua in northern Italy. There students dissected dead bodies to learn anatomy. At the time, the church strongly disapproved of this practice, too. Also at Padua, Italian doctors discovered that blood circulates between the heart and the lungs.

THE END OF THE RENAISSANCE

Golden ages, unfortunately, never last long. The European Renaissance, triggered by Italy, spanned three hundred years. Bitter warfare finally extinguished its brilliant light.

Art continued to develop after the Renaissance. A period known as the baroque era flourished from the late 1500s through the 1700s. Baroque painters, sculptors, and architects hoped to achieve more excitement and drama through elaborate decoration than had the masters of the Renaissance. Art historians still debate the worth of baroque art as compared to Renaissance art.

The warfare that shook Europe came as a reaction against the powerful Roman Catholic church. Over the centuries, the office of the pope had grown corrupt. High positions in church government were bought and sold by ambitious priests. In 1517, a German priest named Martin Luther drew up a list of church reforms. He nailed that list to a church door. His act began the period in history known as the Protestant Reformation. Northern Europe became divided between Catholics and Protestants. A series of religious wars broke out in Germany. The ideas of the Reformation were not accepted by Italians, and the country remained Catholic. But the wars and tensions caused by the Reformation broke the spirit of the Renaissance.

Three hundred years of high culture left a mark on Italy that has never been erased, however. Dozens of Italian cities and towns owe their loveliness largely to Renaissance architects. In museums throughout the world hang priceless paintings by Italian Renaissance masters. Today every Italian carries a sense of pride for the miracles achieved by their countrymen during that golden age called the Renaissance.

Until the early nineteenth century, regionalism was an ingrained
Italian trait. Residents of Florence (above) and Volterra (below),
for instance, considered themselves Tuscans, rather than Italians.

Chapter 4
THE PAINFUL ROAD
TO UNITY

Wars in northern Europe often spilled over into Italy. Conquering armies found the land easy prey because the Italian people had no sense of nation. Italian states and city-states were so jealous of their independence that they often refused to help one another when one was under attack. This situation made Italy militarily the weakest area in Europe. From 1500 to 1800, parts of Italy were occupied by foreign powers almost continuously.

THE HIGH COST OF REGIONALISM

Until the early nineteenth century, patriotism to an Italian was a grudging loyalty to a region or state. A person from the region of Tuscany would say, "I am a Tuscan." An Italian from the state of Lombardy was "a Lombard." No one would admit to being "an Italian." To a certain extent, that ingrained regionalism haunts Italy even today.

This regionalism did far more than make the country militarily weak. Regionalism also prevented Italy from experiencing political progress. In other parts of Europe, poor people began to demand a better way of life. But in Italy, powerful landlords continued to hold an iron grip over their landless peasants.

Regionalism made conducting business in Italy a nightmare. Each state had its own currency, its own system of weights and measures, its own taxes. A barge carrying goods down the Po River had to pay taxes at twenty-two different customs stops. And each state spoke a different dialect, making business transactions even more difficult.

Then two events contributed to the seemingly impossible goal of Italian unity. First, the young United States declared its independence from Great Britain. This proved to Italian nationalists that a weak but determined people could defeat a political giant. Second, in 1789, a mighty revolution broke out in neighboring France.

THE FRENCH REVOLUTION AND ITALY

The French lower classes rose up against the rich landlords who had ruled them for centuries. They also forced their king off his throne and created a republic, as had the Romans two thousand years earlier.

The excitement of the French Revolution spread to Italy. Secret clubs, composed of those who wanted to depose the noblemen in power, looked to the French for help.

Soon the armies of the new French republic began to sweep across Europe. Led by Napoleon Bonaparte, the French marched into northern Italy and expelled the Austrian soldiers who had been occupying the country. The republicans of Italy greeted Napoleon as a conquering hero.

This famous painting of Napoleon Bonaparte crossing the Alps is an oil by Jacques Louis David

Starting in 1796, the French Revolutionary government in Italy ruled for twenty years. Ultimately, Napoleon helped the Italians down their rugged road toward unity. For the first time since ancient Rome, the entire Italian peninsula was ruled by one governing body. For the first time, each state in the country used the same set of laws. And under French rule, regional princes were deposed and local republics were established.

In 1815, Napoleon was defeated at the Battle of Waterloo. Anti-republican countries reestablished the old regional princes in Italy. Austria once again occupied the northern half of the peninsula.

The dream of a republican form of government did not fade among Italian patriots, however. But they had no leadership. Then, by an amazing stroke of fortune, they got not one dynamic leader, but three.

RISORGIMENTO

The three leaders of the Italian struggle to create a united nation shared a fanatical devotion to their cause. Other than that, it would be difficult to imagine three more dissimilar men. Camillo Benso, Conte di Cavour, was a suave, educated aristocrat. Giuseppe Garibaldi had first gone to sea as a sailor at the age of fifteen. Giuseppe Mazzini was a lawyer from a middle-class family. During the struggle for unification, the three men grew to mistrust and even to hate one another. Yet none wavered in his determination to forge one Italy from a dozen different states.

Giuseppe Mazzini was thin, frail, and sickly. He was also a dreamer. Mazzini envisioned an era of peace and progress for all of Europe in which poverty was eliminated and the lowliest peasant could enjoy freedom and security. Although he belonged to no church, Mazzini was said to be mystical in his religious devotion. But he was practical enough to know that ideals were useless unless they could be converted into action.

In 1831, Mazzini organized a group called *Giovane Italia* ("Young Italy"). It favored the unification of Italy and opposed the powers of local dukes, princes, and landlords. Mazzini told his followers they had a religious duty to rise up and proclaim a new age. Because of his radical views, Mazzini spent much of his adult life in exile.

Most of Mazzini's beliefs went into a newsletter he called *Risorgimento* ("rebirth," or "resurrection"). For Italian patriots, risorgimento became a spiritual battle cry of a new, united Italy.

First, however, the Austrian army had to be driven out of the country. This was accomplished largely through the diplomatic genius of Conte di Cavour. Cavour served as prime minister under the king of the island nation of Sardinia. In 1858, he made an alliance with the French leader Napoleon III, a distant cousin of Napoleon Bonaparte. This was a brilliant move that forced Austria to declare war on France and Sardinia. Cavour believed that his side could win such a war, and he was correct. In quick order, French and Sardinian soldiers pushed the Austrian army out of northern Italy. Meanwhile, local peasants rose up to expel local dukes and princes. By 1866, all of northern Italy was united under the king of Sardinia.

Next, Italian partiots cast their eyes to the south. For centuries, a nation called the Kingdom of the Two Sicilies had ruled the south of Italy and the island of Sicily. Often invaded and occupied by foreigners, it remained a land of repression and feudalism. The landowners lived like kings. Patriot Giuseppe Garibaldi hoped to break their power.

Garibaldi today remains Italy's most popular folk hero. In the south he is still thought of as a delivering saint. Always a man of action, Garibaldi was barely out of his teens when he led a revolt against a local king. The uprising failed and Garibaldi fled to South America. There he joined other republican causes, always on the side of the lower classes. During these revolutions, he discovered that he had a particular genius for guerrilla warfare. His electric speaking voice could turn trembling young men into fearless soldiers. So dynamic was his leadership that when he returned to Italy, men came from far-off lands to join his army.

In 1860, Garibaldi landed in Sicily with about a thousand soldiers. From then on, his band was called *I Mille* ("the thousand"). His men wore uniforms with flaming red shirts. The long-suffering peasants of Sicily greeted Garibaldi and his "thousand red shirts" as saviors. Aided by the peasants, Garibaldi

Giuseppe Garibaldi, one of the leaders in the fight to unite Italy, is the country's most popular folk hero.

defeated the Kingdom of the Two Sicilies, and quickly swept over the island. His forces, swollen with local volunteers, next crossed the Strait of Messina and landed on the southern tip of the Italian boot. Once more acclaimed as a liberator by the peasants, Garibaldi marched into Naples, the capital of the old kingdom. The onetime king fled the country.

Garibaldi hoped to continue his march north, conquer the Papal States, and make a triumpant entrance into Rome. But Rome was occupied by French soldiers. France was afraid to have a suddenly united Italy as a neighbor. The pope also supported the French army in Rome, fearing that a new government would weaken the church.

Then a war between France and Prussia drew away most of the French soldiers from Rome. In 1870, an Italian army was able to seize the now vulnerable city.

The forces of risorgimento had won. At last Italy was a united country.

Rome became the capital of the new Italy. The Roman Catholic church, once a mighty landowner, saw its properties reduced to Vatican City, a 108-acre (44-hectare) site in the center of Rome. Pope Pius IX refused to recognize the new government of Italy, starting a feud between government and church that lasted for decades.

To the dismay of many, the new government of Italy was not a republic. Instead, the king of Sardinia became the king of Italy. But this king, Victor Emmanuel II, accepted the spirit of risorgimento. And Sardinia had been a leader in the push for Italian unification. For these reasons, most Italian republicans, including Garibaldi, grudgingly accepted the establishment of a monarchy. The antimonarchy patriots consoled themselves with one fact: For the first time since the Roman Empire, the Italian peninsula was united under the leadership of an Italian.

THE KINGDOM OF ITALY

Author and politician Massimo d'Azeglio wrote: "We have made Italy, now we have to make Italians." This would be no easy task. Centuries of regionalism had created a mentality that would not change simply because a new government declared Italy to be united.

Many factors combined to keep regionalism a strong force. One was centuries of pure habit. Another was the ancient division

These families about to disembark at Ellis Island were among the millions of people who left Italy during the late 1800s and early 1900s.

between the rich north and the poor south. Northern Italians had led the struggle for unification and now dominated the new government. This led southern Italians to believe the new government was indifferent to their needs. The pope also created divisions. Enraged over the loss of church property, he forbade Catholics to participate in the new government. Many Catholics, however, ignored their pope's orders.

The new Italian kingdom also suffered from a lack of industrialization. Other European countries were busy building factories; Italy remained mired in feudalism. Catching up with modern Europe would be a monumental task.

As the twentieth century approached, massive emigrations left a greater mark on Italy than a change in government had done. To escape grinding poverty, Italians began to move to the United States and Latin America. Most of the emigrants were from southern Italy. Many built comfortable lives in their new lands. Their letters home encouraged others to try their luck abroad. Between 1887 and 1900, half a million people left Italy each year. And the trend continued well into the twentieth century. In 1913 alone, 872,000 Italians sailed from their native land.

This population drain eased some of Italy's poverty. Still, Italy's most severe problems were yet to surface.

Chapter 5

ITALY ENTERS THE MODERN WORLD

Italians enjoy art and music that is grand in scale. They are the inventors of grand opera. Grand operas have lavish sets and call for scores of performers. In some productions, horses and even elephants climb onto the stage. Italian leaders carried their love for this kind of grandeur into the twentieth century. They pursued a foreign policy designed to build a magnificent new empire. Sadly, their foreign adventures left Italy heaped in ashes.

Giuseppe Verdi (1813-1901) was a great composer of Italian grand opera. When he died, an eighteen-year old student delivered a tearful commemoration for the beloved composer in a small-town theater. People in the audience were moved by the young man's powerful speaking voice. They took note of his name, because many believed he was destined for success. The student's name was Benito Mussolini.

"Italy must not only be respected, she must make herself feared," King Victor Emmanuel II proclaimed at the turn of the century. For hundreds of years, other important European countries had claimed colonies throughout the world. But Italy,

These Italian troops were making camp in Tripoli after seizing the country in 1911.

which lacked a central government, had no colonies at all. The new government was determined to make up for lost time.

Initially, Italy turned to North Africa. It grabbed Tripoli as a colonial prize, after winning a war against Turkey in 1911. In 1914, World War I broke out in Europe. For the first year of the war, Italy remained neutral. Then the Allied governments promised Italy a huge chunk of European territory if she would declare war on the Central Powers. Hungry for expansion, Italy sided with the Allies and entered the fighting in 1915.

The Italian leadership plunged into the war with great expectations. But the Italian military was woefully unprepared to face the new and terrible weapons—machine guns, poison gas, and rapid-firing artillery. After four years of fighting, Italy had suffered more than two million casualties.

At war's end, Italy did not receive all the territory promised by the victorious Allies. And the economic cost of the war left the country heavily in debt. Italians entered the postwar period staggered by their loss of young men, nearly bankrupt, and frustrated because few of their territorial dreams had been fulfilled. A change of government was in order. Most Italians wanted a strong, dynamic leader who could patch together their crippled country. So they began listening to the fiery speeches of a man who headed the new Fascist political party.

BENITO MUSSOLINI

Benito Mussolini was born in Forli Province in 1883. His father was a political visionary who worked as a blacksmith. Young Benito Mussolini grew up a Socialist. Because of his father's sacrifices, he was able to attend college. After graduation, he taught in a primary school and then worked as a laborer in Switzerland. There he often got into fistfights while preaching socialism to other workers. When he returned to Italy, he founded a newspaper, *Il Popolo D'Italia.* He was expelled from the Socialist party because his newspaper favored Italy's entry into the war against the Germans.

After World War I, Mussolini's politics changed dramatically. In 1919, he formed what he called the Fascist party. Fascists were anti-Socialist, anti-Communist, and anti-labor. Mussolini played on the fears of both the middle class and the wealthy by warning of a soon-to-come Communist revolution. He insisted that order must be maintained in Italy even if that meant curtailing people's rights. Acting out of fear, wealthy people poured money into the Fascist party's treasury.

*In 1922, Fascist leader
Benito Mussolini (right)
was made premier by King
Victor Emmanuel III (left).*

The party grew in membership and might. Many members were war veterans, discontented because Italy had not obtained all the territory promised them before World War I.

The years 1919 to 1922 were troubled times for Italy. Labor strikes paralyzed factories and railroads. Runaway inflation wiped out people's savings. Membership in the Italian Communist party soared.

Many Italians saw Mussolini as a hero who would save their country from the godless Communists. By 1922, the Fascists had become powerful enough politically that King Victor Emmanuel III, worried about civil disorder, called on Mussolini to run the government. Within three years, Mussolini was ruling Italy as a dictator. He took the title *Il Duce* ("the leader").

ITALY UNDER THE FASCISTS

The word *fascism* comes from an ancient Roman symbol of authority called *fasces*. Mussolini coined the word when he formed his political party. Fascists believed in a one-man, ironhanded rule, and a suppression of civil rights.

Fascism quickly crept into every corner of Italian life. Opposition political parties were prohibited. Socialists were sent into domestic exile. Labor leaders were forced to pledge loyalty to the government. The radio and newspaper used propaganda skillfully to extol the progress of the Mussolini government. Schoolchildren were organized into marching societies (*balilla*) and paraded through the streets carrying banners that hailed Fascist rule.

In Germany, a young Adolf Hitler was overcome with admiration as he read of Mussolini's success. Hitler headed the National Socialists, a fledgling political group that also embraced the principles of fascism.

One-man rule often can accomplish feats that democratic government cannot manage. The Italian national budget was balanced and inflation was halted. Mussolini ordered large-scale public works, such as the building of bridges and the draining of swamps. Since labor unions were controlled and strikes were prohibited, work on these projects ran smoothly. For the first time in memory, trains in Italy ran on time. Mussolini also poured money into armaments, especially building up Italy's navy. One of his accomplishments was the 1929 Lateran Treaty. It made Vatican City a separate state and ended the sixty-year-old feud between the Italian government and the Roman Catholic church. (The treaty was revised in 1984.)

Mussolini promised that Italy would rise again to rival the glory of Rome. That meant Italy must have its own empire. Colonies, he hoped, would keep the economy prosperous. To acquire them, the nation had to wage war. It did, almost constantly from 1935 to 1945.

On October 3, 1935, Italian troops landed on the shores of Ethiopia in northern Africa. A terrible war broke out, pitting Italian soldiers armed with machine guns and artillery against very poorly armed Ethiopians. When Ethiopia finally succumbed, *Il Duce* announced to the world that a new Roman Empire had risen.

Italy's bloody conquest of Ethiopia outraged world leaders. Mussolini became an outcast in Europe. Consequently, he was pushed closer toward Europe's other outcast—Adolf Hitler. The two signed a friendship agreement in 1936.

ITALY DURING WORLD WAR II

On September 1, 1939, Germany invaded Poland, plunging Europe into World War II. For the first nine months of the war, Italy stayed out of the fighting. Mussolini watched jealously as Hitler overran Poland, Denmark, and Norway. When France, too, was almost defeated, Italy entered the war on Germany's side.

Envious of Hitler's military successes, Mussolini attacked Greece in October, 1940, thinking that country would be easy prey. But Italy's war machine was not as brutally efficient as Germany's. The army was unprepared for battle. Greek soldiers fought with heroic stubbornness and stopped the Italian advance. To aid his Fascist partner and to gobble up more territory for himself, Hitler attacked Yugoslavia and continued his sweep south until Greece fell.

From 1926 to 1943, Mussolini (shown at right with Adolf Hitler) addressed huge Fascist crowds from the balcony of his residence, the Palazzo Venezia (left).

Meanwhile, Italy suffered setbacks in its North African colonies. The British army seized both Libya (formerly Tripoli) and the newly won Ethiopia. Once more, Hitler had to bail Mussolini out of trouble. He sent to North Africa a combined German-Italian army called the Afrika Korps. A period of wild tank warfare between the British army and the Afrika Korps raged across the North African desert. The British were joined by American units late in 1942. The once invincible Afrika Korps was forced to surrender to the Allies.

Following their victory in North Africa, the Allies invaded and occupied Sicily in July of 1943. This put Italian cities within range of Allied bombers.

In Italy, morale sagged. The people blamed Mussolini for the disastrous string of defeats. *Il Duce* was arrested by members of his own party and exiled on a secluded mountain . King Victor Emmanuel III tried to make a separate peace with the Allies, but German troops poured into the peninsula from the north. The Italians, once partners with the Germans, now became their captives.

The Allies invaded Italy in September, 1943, and were met by German troops solidly dug in on Italy's rugged mountains. Italy became a terrible battleground and remained one until the end of the war. Bloody battles were fought at Anzio and Monte Cassino. Many of the Allied troops who fought and died in these battles were Italian-Americans—sons and grandsons of Italians who had emigrated to America.

A daring German parachute raid rescued Mussolini from his mountain prison. He was flown to northern Italy, which was under German occupation. But German forces in northern Italy collapsed in the spring of 1945. Italian freedom fighters discovered Mussolini and his girl friend Clara Petacci at their mountain hideout. The two were shot. Their bodies were taken to the city of Milan, where townspeople hung them upside down by their feet.

At one time, Mussolini had promised to make Italy great. Now the stones pelting against his lifeless body sounded the final notes of his sorry adventure in power.

THE ITALIAN REPUBLIC

At the end of the war, many proud old Italian cities lay in ashes. Hunger and disease swept the population. The nation had no effective government. Once more, Italy was occupied by foreign soldiers.

At the end of World War II, many proud old Italian towns (including Castelforte, above) lay in ruins.

The Allies hammered out the terms of a peace treaty and the nation's leaders were forced to accept them. Italy lost all her foreign colonies, and some of her European territory was awarded to Yugoslavia. In addition, Italy was stripped of her military and forced to pay some war reparations.

The war left Italians with bitter feelings toward fascism. During the party's rule, the king was closely associated with the Fascists. In 1946, voters ousted the king and established a republic. Italy has remained a republic since then.

Italians today, at work and play:
Two Venetian children (above) cuddle
their cat, a favorite pet in Venice;
a Palermo woman (above right) hangs out
her wash; a father and his son (below)
read the morning newspapers in Rome;
and a fisherman repairs a net (right).

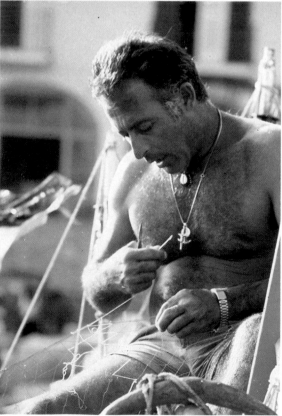

Chapter 6

CHALLENGES FOR
TODAY'S ITALY

Like the rest of Europe, Italy began a long, painful economic recovery after World War II. American aid, granted under the Marshall Plan, helped. The most powerful postwar figure in Italy was Alcide De Gasperi, head of the Christian Democratic party and premier from 1945 to 1953. Under his leadership, Italy formed closer ties with western Europe and the United States. In 1950, Italy became one of the founding members of the European mutual defense pact called the North Atlantic Treaty Organization (NATO).

From its beginnings as a republic, Italy has had to cope with a jumble of political parties. On election day, as many as fifteen parties present candidates. Never once have the Italians given a majority of votes to any one party. In 1976, for example, the Christian Democrats received 38.7 percent of the vote, the Communists 34.4 percent, and the Socialists 9.6 percent. The rest of the vote was divided among a score of lesser parties.

The Christian Democrats have led the country's parliament since the 1940s. The party has formed coalitions, or alliances, with both left-wing (liberal or radical) and right-wing (conservative) groups. By remaining flexible, the Christian Democrats have maintained their general popularity, their power, and the approval of the Catholic church.

In the 1960s, the Italian economy began to boom. Italian products—everything from sports cars to leather goods to olive oil—were in demand abroad. But then the economy, like that of so many other nations, suffered a sharp slowdown. Unemployment was complicated by inflation, which was caused largely by climbing energy costs. Many blamed the economic woes on the Christian Democratic party.

During the 1970s, the power of the Italian Communists grew. Always the country's second largest vote-getter, the party saw its membership increase as Italy's economy turned sour.

THE WORKING GOVERNMENT

Italy has a vast welfare system that includes subsidized medical care, unemployment compensation, and old-age pensions. A system of family allowances helps the very poor. Critics complain, however, that welfare grants are inadequate and that public health care is of poor quality. Still, the welfare system has eased the extremes of poverty.

Today Italy is the sixth leading industrial nation in the world. Manufacturing employs almost 30 percent of the work force. Italy exports billions of dollars worth of trucks, cars, motor scooters, and tractors. The textile and wine industries also are important. The country is one of the largest exporters of wine in the world. Tourism has always been and continues to be a major source of income for Italy.

The Ricasoli family, winemakers since 1141, have made a major contribution to the growth of the Italian wine industry. Their Brolio winery (above) developed the famous Chianti Classico, with a rooster on the bottle neck, in the 1840s.

Despite the country's considerable economic success, unemployment and inflation remained nagging problems in the 1980s. Many unemployed and underemployed workers joined the "underground economy," bartering homemade goods or their labor for cash or products they needed. Many of Italy's talented craftsmen make their living this way. The government frowns on the underground economy because its participants pay no taxes.

In foreign policy, the Italian government usually takes a pro-Western stand. Historically, Italy has been one of America's best friends in Europe. In 1983, the government sent Italian troops to Lebanon to support American and French forces in their peace-keeping operation. But when it became clear that the foreign soldiers could not keep the peace in that war-torn land, Italy pulled out its forces and urged the United States to do the same.

Most citizens take a lively interest in the complexities of Italian politics. But a tiny minority disdain the give-and-take process that takes place in parliament. They believe that the political system must be destroyed before it can be rebuilt effectively.

This Red Brigade snapshot showing NATO General James L. Dozier was left in a Milan trash can before Dozier was rescued from the terrorists after forty-two days in captivity.

THE TERRORISTS

Italian terrorists are tiny groups of men and women who use violence to advance their political causes. Although these groups receive an enormous amount of news coverage, they actually number only a few hundred. Public-opinion polls show that nearly all Italians disapprove of their activities.

The terrorists are opposed to all political parties. They operate in secret, and represent both the extreme political left and the right. They plant bombs, kidnap some people, and gun down others. A major terrorist group in Italy is a leftist organization called the Red Brigade. In 1978, the Red Brigade kidnapped and killed Italian ex-premier Aldo Moro. Moro was expected to become the next Italian president. In 1981, terrorists kidnapped United States Brigadier General James Dozier, a NATO commander. However, after forty-two days in captivity, Dozier was rescued by an elite squad of Italian police specially trained in antiterrorist tactics.

Even though inflation in Italy raced along at about 25 per cent a year in the 1980s, and the number of unemployed grew steadily, the people remained friendly and gracious.

Extremists on the right also turn to terrorism. In fact, it is estimated that right-wing guerrillas were responsible for 132 of the 250 terrorist murders committed during the 1970s. A shocking example of right-wing terrorism took place on August 2, 1980. A powerful bomb blew up the Bologna railroad station and killed eighty people, most of whom were innocent vacationers. A neo-Fascist group called the Armed Revolutionary Nuclei claimed to have set the bomb.

THE INDOMITABLE ITALIAN SPIRIT

In Italy during the early 1980s, inflation raced along at about 25 percent a year, and the number of unemployed grew steadily. Yet the people remained as friendly and as gracious as ever. Italian men and women have had crises in the past, but the indomitable Italian spirit has always pulled them through. It will, no doubt, enable Italy to survive any current crisis, as well.

*Italian teams play soccer, the country's most popular spectator sport,
at the Siena municipal soccer field against the town's medieval skyline.*

Chapter 7

ITALIANS AT EASE

Italians are among the hardest working people on earth. Visitors to the country marvel at the tireless determination of Italian workers. Because of their driving energy, many poor Italian men and women who emigrated to the United States rose to the middle class. Some even became millionaires.

But Italians love their leisure time, too. That same boundless energy spurs them to creative heights during off-hours. They approach both leisure and work with enthusiam and the joy of being alive.

SPORTS AND GAMES

Sports are a passion in Italy. Anything from bicycle racing to boxing draws huge, wildly cheering crowds. Italy's great athletes are highly paid, idolized heroes.

Soccer is the most popular spectator sport. Every large city has a team that competes in a league. Major soccer games are played to sellout crowds. Olympic Stadium in Rome often draws 100,000 fans for a soccer match.

Ancient Italian regionalism can bleed over into the sports

The Italian mania for soccer and love of betting go hand in hand. Billions of lire (left) are wagered in the weekly soccer pool, and the Olympic Stadium in Rome (right) draws huge crowds for the soccer matches held from September to June.

stadium. Fistfights sometimes break out in the stands. On some occasions, fights have snowballed into rioting and gunfire. But once every four years, all Italian soccer fans cheer for the same team. That occurs when Italy's national team competes in the international World Cup games. All of Italy held its breath when the Italian team played against West Germany in the 1982 finals. In a thrilling contest, the Italian team won. The nation went wild! Some celebration parties lasted for weeks.

Professional basketball is another popular team sport in Italy. Most Italian pro teams feature two or three Americans who are perhaps just a step too slow to star in America. Italians are also devoted to bicycle racing. Italian cyclists usually do well in the Olympics. Auto racing has a wide following, too. A round-the-island race in Sicily has been held each year since 1906.

Many varieties of Italian cheese and sausage are famous the world over.

Directly related to the Italian mania for sports is their love of betting. In the government's weekly soccer pool (called *Totocalcio*), billions of lire (Italian money) are wagered. The government also sponsors a national lottery based on the familiar game of lotto. It is believed that lotto was invented in Genoa some three hundred years ago.

In village squares, card games are played on outdoor benches all summer long. The participants—usually retired men—slap winning cards onto the table with knuckle-shattering force. A favorite Sunday morning game—again often played by older men—is called *bocce*. It is a form of lawn bowling using wooden balls.

FOOD AND FESTIVALS

Everybody loves Italian food—spaghetti, pizza, and lasagna instantly come to mind. But Italian food is infinitely more varied. Regionalism, in the case of cooking, has produced pleasant results.

Before the wild horse race held in Siena's Piazza del Campo during the Palio festival, townspeople dressed in costumes of the Middle Ages parade through the town. This carriage is displaying the race winner's prize, a banner with the image of the Madonna.

Some regional culinary treats: in Bologna, *tortellini*, little rounds of dough stuffed with cheese and meat; in Rome, *abacchio al forno*, roast lamb spiced with rosemary; on the island of Sardinia, *buridda*, a fish soup; and in Sicily, *maccheroni con le sarde*, macaroni with a sardine sauce. Bread and wine, the heart and soul of Italy, are taken with every meal.

Some critics believe one of the reasons for ancient Rome's decline was that too many holidays were celebrated each year. Holidays in present-day Italy can be religious, patriotic, or regional affairs. Many date back to Roman times.

Christmas is both a solemn and a happy occasion. Several days before Christmas, a nativity scene called a *presepio* is set up inside every Italian church and in most private homes. A *presepio* is a group of carved wooden figures that represent the Holy Family, the shepherds, the three Wise Men, and the stable animals. Some families display *presepios* so large they take up half the living room.

The Palio *horse race is held in the Piazza del Campo, Siena's beautiful medieval fan-shaped square (left).*

Nine days before Christmas Eve, bagpipers (yes!) perform in the streets of Italian villages from morning to night. In Italy, families exchange gifts on the Feast of Epiphany, twelve days after Christmas.

An important patriotic holiday falls on April 25. That day is the anniversary of the 1944 liberation of Italy from German occupation.

Each region has a special festival day. Some festivals honor the feast day of a town's patron saint. Others might commemorate a historic event whose roots have long been forgotten.

One popular regional festival is the *Palio*, which takes place twice a year in Siena, a marvelous hill town some forty miles (sixty-four kilometers) south of Florence. The *Palio* begins with a parade of townspeople dressed in costumes of the Middle Ages. Some of the men wear ancient suits of armor that glitter brightly in the sun. The *Palio* ends with a wild horse race around the tiny town square. Running at breakneck speed, through ninety-degree turns, horses often throw off their jockeys. The winner's cup goes to the horse that finishes first, whether or not it still has a rider.

The island of Burano (above) is the center of the Venetian lace-making industry.
The Venetian lace maker shown below is demonstrating her art at a craft show.

ARTS AND CRAFTS

Not all art is displayed in museums. Italians are splendid craftsmen. Their handiwork is both a leisure-time activity and a commercial enterprise.

Near the city of Venice lies the island of Murano. Master glassblowers of Murano create strikingly beautiful goblets and bowls. And for centuries, they have made tiny glass beads that look like pearls. It is said that the glass beads used by the Dutch to buy Manhattan from the American Indians were made on Murano. For generations, families on the island have handed down glassblowing skills from father to son. As recently as two hundred years ago, a Murano glassmaker who revealed his trade secrets to an outsider could be put to death.

Italy is also world famous for its leather products. In small workshops dotting the countryside, skilled men and women fashion leather into belts, shoes, handbags, and gloves. These handmade leather goods are sold in Italian villages at moderate prices. But they carry whopping prices in the best shops of New York and Paris.

Lace making is a craft practiced mostly by Italian women living in small mountain villages. Their work is so delicate that a magnifying glass is needed to see all the intricate details.

MUSIC

From beloved folk songs to magnificent operas, Italian music is known worldwide. Through the ages music, like art, has been one of Italy's greatest exports.

From their earliest history, Italians have been leaders in the

Enrico Caruso, who had the most beautiful operatic tenor voice in the history of music, is shown here in costume for his role in Verdi's opera Rigoletto.

world of classical music. Even its language comes from the Italian. The word *solo*, as in playing a solo instrument, is the Italian word meaning "alone." In classical music, a fast movement is an *allegro* and an even faster one is a *presto*. Both words are from the Italian, meaning "happy" and "quick." The names of many instruments—piano, violin, and cello, for instance—were all originally Italian.

Rock music is popular among Italian teenagers. Folk songs and folk dances are popular, too, especially in the villages. But Italy's triumph in music is the opera.

Opera was born in Italy with the first performance of *Eurydice*, by Jacopo Peri, in 1600. In 1607, Italian Claudio Monteverdi wrote *Orfeo*, which many historians consider to be the world's first opera masterpiece. Even the word *opera* ("a work") comes from the Italian. Italian operagoers are very critical of a performance. They cheer wildly for a brilliant rendition and boo relentlessly for a bad one. They once booed history's greatest tenor, Enrico Caruso, off the stage because he missed a high note.

La Scala, in Milan, is probably the most famous opera house in the world.

Some of the most famous composers of opera were Italians. In the early 1800s, Gioacchino Rossini (1792-1868) thrilled music lovers with his sparkling opera *The Barber of Seville* and Gaetano Donizetti (1797-1848) wrote his famous *Don Pasquale*. Giuseppe Verdi (1813-1901) wrote grand operas that called for dozens of performers and elaborate stage settings. Verdi's most famous works include *Rigoletto, La Traviata, Aida,* and *Otello.* Giacomo Puccini (1858-1924) is best known for *La Boheme, Tosca, Madame Butterfly,* and *Turandot.*

Opera is a special form of theater in which people sing, rather than speak, their lines. Italian operas, especially, tell stories that are highly dramatic and complicated by love, murder, and intrigue. As a plot unfolds, an orchestra plays somber or triumphant music to fit the mood of each scene. A chorus of many singers may join the orchestra. Exquisite duets and solos are performed by the leading singers. It all adds up to dramatic excitement that makes Italian opera loved everywhere in the world.

Not all Italian composers of classical music wrote opera. Antonio Vivaldi (1678-1741) and Niccoló Paganini (1782-1840) wrote instrumental music. Vivaldi's most popular work is the *Four Seasons*, which gives impressions of the physical and spiritual changes a person feels as the seasons shift from spring to summer, and from fall to winter. Paganini was not only a composer, but also such a marvelous violinist that a fantastic story spread about his talent. It was whispered that Paganini had made a deal with the devil in exchange for his superhuman talent as a violinist. A later Italian composer of instrumental music was Ottorino Respighi (1879-1936). Among his works are two marvelous tone poems — *The Pines of Rome* and *The Fountains of Rome* — written about the city he loved.

Modern music blares from radios on city streets. One famous singer, Pino Daniele, is often called the "Bob Dylan of Italian music." Even the country's popular music, however, maintains a distinctive Italian flair.

LITERATURE

Throughout history, the ideas of great authors have helped mold the Italian character. And from the Renaissance to modern times, Italian authors have won the respect of world audiences. Since the Nobel Prize for literature was first presented in 1901, five Italians have won the coveted prize: Giosue Carducci, 1906, for his poetry; Grazia Deledda, 1926, for her novels; Luigi Pirandello, 1934, plays; Salvatore Quasimodo, 1959, poetry; and Eugenio Montale, 1975, poetry.

Since the Renaissance, the themes of Italian literature have reflected, and in many cases led, shifts in the country's history.

When Italy was dominated by powerful—mostly foreign—noblemen, brave Italian writers attacked the system and often went to prison for it. During the excitement of the risorgimento, nationalistic writers became heroes. Poet Giuseppe Giusti ridiculed foreign leaders and their Italian puppets in his verse. Luigi Mercantini wrote poems and hymns praising Garibaldi. Under Mussolini, anti-Fascist writers were forced into exile. Carlo Levi, banished to a small town in southern Italy, wrote *Christ Stopped at Eboli,* a novel about impoverished conditions there. Published in 1946, it had a great impact during the postwar years. Ignazio Silone also was exiled by the Fascists. His famous novel *Pane e Vino (Bread and Wine)* tells the grim story of peasant farmers in the grip of rich landlords. In the 1960s, Leonardo Sciascia of Sicily wrote novels about the people of his native island.

FILM

The end of World War II unlocked the imagination of the country's filmmakers. In the 1940s, Italian directors launched a new era in films. The first of the films was *Roma, Città Aperta (Open City)*. It told a story of people of the city of Rome in the closing days of the German occupation. Directed by Roberto Rossellini, *Open City* was shot in 1945 when film was scarce, experienced actors were hard to find, and money for sets hardly existed. Rosellini turned these shortcomings into assets. With unpolished, stark realism, he gave a brutally honest account of the Roman people's attempt to start life anew. The film won international praise. Because it was so boldly realistic, it began a new school of neo-realistic movies.

Italian movie actresses Gina Lollobrigida (left) and Sophia Loren (right)

The most famous film of the neo-realism school was the 1948 masterpiece *The Bicycle Thief*. Directed by Vittorio De Sica, the film concerns a man and his young son who roam the streets searching for the father's stolen bicycle. Without the bicycle, the man has no job. In desperation, he steals an unguarded bicycle. He is caught and beaten by an angry crowd. The film ends with the degraded father sitting on the sidewalk holding his son's hand. *The Bicycle Thief* is consistently voted one of the best movies ever made. Its simple, yet moving, story is a superb example of neo-realism. At the time, Hollywood films featured larger-than-life heroes. The neo-realists, on the other hand, showed the triumphs and tragedies of everyday people.

In the 1950s, Italian film personalities gained international fame. Movies starring actresses such as Anna Magnani, Sophia Loren, Gina Lollobrigida, and Silvana Mangano played to worldwide audiences and earned millions of dollars. Federico Fellini began directing movies that dazzled audiences in Europe and America. Fellini soon turned from neo-realism to romanticism. His most famous film, *La Dolce Vita (The Sweet Life)*

Rome's Via Veneto is filmmaker Federico Fellini's "dolce vita" street.

(1959), is a surrealistic look at the life of the superrich in Rome. Other Fellini favorites are *La Strada* (1954), *Juliet of the Spirits* (1966), and *Satyricon* (1969).

PEOPLE WATCHING

In an Italian village it is easy to find the center of town. Look for an old narrow street and follow it until it becomes even narrower and older looking. Invariably, that street will lead to the piazza, or town square. It is usually in the oldest section of town, and the city hall and main church stand there. Ringing the piazza are restaurants, coffee houses, and shops. The piazza itself is a paved, treelined plaza with a statue or a fountain in the middle. It is the heart and soul of any village. And it is the headquarters for people watching.

People watching in the piazza is a marvelous Italian pastime. Villagers sit on benches in the shade, read newspapers, gossip, and watch other people doing exactly the same things.

Piazzas are town centers. City neighborhoods also have piazzas, including Italy's most famous cities.

One of the many canals of Venice is seen here at dusk. The campanile of the Church of Santa Maria della Salute can be seen in the background.

Chapter 8

ITALY'S FAMOUS CITIES

Italy is one of the most-visited countries in Europe. It has breathtaking natural beauty and facilities for both the sun-worshipper and the skier. It is the capital of the Roman Catholic world. But most of all, Italy has cities where all of Western history is frozen in the stone of buildings and monuments. This quick survey of some of those cities begins in the north.

VENICE

Venice is one of the planet's loveliest cities. It is built primarily on some 120 tiny islands that hug the Adriatic coast. Those islands were settled during the fifth century A.D. by Romans fleeing barbarian invasions. The invaders had no boats, so the settlers were safe on the islands. Soon Venice became an important city-state and the capital of the region called Venetia. Venetians were known as superb sailors—the great explorer-sailor Marco Polo was a Venetian. Venice was also an important port during the Crusades. The city grew rich largely from the profits of foreign trade. Many of Venice's finest buildings rose during the

Among the "streets" of Venice are narrow lanes such as this one and the Grand Canal (above right), which is the city's main street.

Renaissance. Today, those splendid structures attract more than three million visitors each year.

As an island city, Venice has no major streets. More than 150 canals cut through the city to take their place. Some four hundred bridges span the canals. The "main street" of Venice is the Grand Canal, which snakes through the center of town. Neither cars, trucks, nor buses are allowed on the narrow lanes and walkways of Venice. Instead, people get around by riding boats along the spiderweb network of canals. Years ago, flat-bottomed, canoelike gondolas served as the principal water taxis. Each gondola was moved along by a husky gondolier who often sang as he plied his pole. At one time, ten thousand gondolas crammed the canals of Venice. Lovers riding the boats as passengers had a tradition of kissing as they passed underneath each bridge. Today, only a few of the colorful gondolas are left. They have been replaced by large motorboats called *vaparettos*.

Though much of the beauty of Venice derives from the waterways, those same waterways have created a major problem for the city. The constant exposure to water and the industrial pollution that has flowed into the canals from Italy's factories have weakened the foundations of the city's buildings.

At the center of Venice lies Saint Mark's Square. Thousands of pigeons come flapping to this piazza each morning to be fed by tourists. Rising above the square is the magnificent Cathedral of Saint Mark. At one time, any citizen of Venice trading with Eastern countries was legally obliged to bring back some treasure to beautify the cathedral. Consequently, magnificent gold work and delicate tile adorn Saint Mark's.

In recent years, Venice has faced a grave threat. Industrial pollution dumped into the Adriatic Sea by northern Italy's many factories has flowed into Venice's canals. The pollutants have weakened the foundations of the city's buildings, many of which are nine hundred years old. Repair crews wage a constant war to patch the foundations and prevent the old buildings from crumbling into the sea.

Jewelry and goldsmith shops line Florence's Ponte Vecchio (above), which spans the Arno River. In the view of the city shown below, the dome of the cathedral dominates the skyline. The great cathedral doors are shown at right.

FLORENCE

The city of Florence (Firenze) is a living museum of the Renaissance. Both Michelangelo and Leonardo da Vinci worked there. Lorenzo de' Medici, the leading Florentine of the time, dreamed of making Florence the most beautiful city in Europe. Venice is the only Italian city that rivals Florence in beauty.

Flowing through the heart of Florence is the Arno River. On the right bank of the river lies the heart of the town—the broad Piazza della Signoria. Nearby the Church of Santa Croce holds the tombs of Galileo, Michelangelo, Machiavelli, and other famous Florentines. Also nearby is the *Galleria dell'Accademia*, which houses Michelangelo's brilliant statue of *David*.

Six bridges span the Arno River along the old section. One of them, the *Ponte Vecchio*, was completed in 1345. Others, quite modern, replace cherished monuments of the Renaissance that were dynamited by retreating German troops in 1945.

In 1966, a disastrous Arno River flood left much of old Florence buried under a layer of mud. Many precious books and paintings were badly damaged. After years of painstaking effort, most of those ancient works have been restored. Progress and prosperity also brought havoc to Florence. In the late 1960s, narrow, tortuous streets of the old section were choked with cars. So, in 1970, city officials banned private automobiles from the historic center of town.

MILAN

Milan, a bustling industrial city of almost two million people, is Italy's second largest city. Busy Milan has high rises, freeways,

Milan's Gothic cathedral

factories, and a frantic pace of life. The city is the headquarters for many of Italy's most powerful corporations. Yet Milan has a well-preserved old section that is a delight to visit.

Music lovers from all over the world flock to hear opera performed at La Scala. Built in 1778, La Scala is probably the most famous opera house in the world.

In the center of the old section is the Milan Cathedral, Europe's third largest church. The building's outside walls are covered with intricate carvings. The Gothic cathedral has 135 marble spires jutting out of its roof. Each spire bears a statue. Near the cathedral stands the Ambrosian Library, a treasure house of rare books. Also nearby is the fortresslike Sforza Castle, which once served

Milan's feudal prince. One of the most famous masterpieces in history—Leornardo da Vinci's fresco *The Last Supper*—can still be seen cn a wall of the Monastery of Santa Maria della Grazie in the old section of Milan.

In northern Italy, there are many more fascinating cities. In Pisa stands the famous Leaning Tower, perhaps the world's most recognized building. In the ancient Mediterranean port of Genoa stands the house where Christopher Columbus was born. Turin, on the Po River, is a lovely town that was captured by the Carthaginian General Hannibal in 218 B.C.

NAPLES

Some 143 miles (230 kilometers) south of Rome lies Naples, a bayside city of pleasant climate year-round. With a population of more than a million, the city is the third largest in the country, and is usually thought of as the capital of southern Italy.

Castles belonging to feudal lords still stand in parts of Naples. The oldest of these, built in the shape of an egg, is called *Castel dell' Ovo* (Castle of the Egg).

From the sea, the city appears to curve around its bay like a huge crescent. Towering above Naples is Mount Vesuvius, the only active volcano on the continent of Europe. Every now and then a wisp of smoke curls from its top, reminding Neapolitans that the volcano is not dead—just sleeping. In the year A.D. 79, Vesuvius erupted and buried the Roman towns of Herculaneum and Pompeii under bubbling lava. Archaeologists are still

A mighty eruption of Mount Vesuvius (background, left) buried Pompeii under tons of lava in 79 A.D. Much of the town has been excavated, and visitors today can see the amphitheater (left) and these frescoes in the House of the Vetti (right).

carefully uncovering those cities, hoping to make discoveries that will broaden ancient Roman history.

Although the people of Naples generally are poorer than people in the north, they somehow seem happier. Singing in public is common in Italy, but in Naples it is universal. Songs fill the neighborhood piazzas at night. Food in Naples is based on inexpensive ingredients, such as macaroni and spaghetti. It is said that a Neapolitan baker invented one of America's favorite foods—pizza—in the early 1700s.

PALERMO

A casual visitor to Italy often fails to include the island of Sicily on his itinerary. This is a mistake.

A favorite meeting place for Romans and tourists alike, the Spanish Steps lead up to the twin-towered Church of the Santissima Trinità dei Monti.

The port city of Palermo is Sicily's capital. The city was founded by the Phoenicians in the 600s B.C. After the Fall of Rome, Palermo was conquered by a parade of different peoples including the Normans. Over the years, many conquerors came and went, leaving a fantastic diversity of architecture behind them. A Norman cathedral built in the twelfth century still stands in Palermo. Many city improvements were made by the remarkable ruler Frederick II, who is buried in the cathedral.

ROME—THE ETERNAL CITY

The visitor to Italy will eventually arrive at its capital, because today, as was true two thousand years ago, all roads lead to Rome.

The piazzas of Rome are adorned with statues, fountains, and monuments. The Piazza Navona holds Bernini's magnificent Fountain of the Four Rivers (left), and the elaborate King Victor Emmanuel II monument stands in the Piazza Venezia.

For lovers of history and art, there are few cities more glorious. A trained eye can read great historical chapters in the city's monuments and buildings.

In ancient times, Rome's boundaries extended over seven hills. Today, the city has sprawled to cover thirteen more. Rome's 1981 population stood at nearly three million.

The Tiber River flows the length of the city. At the center of Rome lies what is sometimes called the Ancient City. Ruins of the mighty Roman Empire still stand there, surrounded by delightful monuments of the Renaissance, baroque, and modern artistic periods.

The piazzas of Rome are adorned with fountains and statues. When the popes ruled Rome, the church spent fortunes decorating

From this outdoor cafe (left) diners can watch the activity in the Piazza Navona. An Egyptian obelisk is the focal point of the oval-shaped Piazza del Popolo (right).

the piazzas to impress visiting pilgrims. Artists such as Michelangelo and Giovanni Lorenzo Bernini were commissioned to design fountains and monuments. Today, they stand like miniature museums along the busy streets.

The Piazza Navona was once the site of Roman chariot racing. It retains the oval shape of a racetrack. One of the three fountains in the piazza was designed by baroque master Bernini. In 1536, Pope Paul III commissioned Michelangelo to lay out and build the Piazza dell Campidoglio. The pavement of the plaza has an enchanting, starlike design. A landmark in Rome is the Piazza di Spagna with its graceful Spanish Steps, a meeting place for Romans and tourists alike.

In the Piazza Venezia stands the elaborate marble "wedding cake" monument erected to honor King Victor Emmanuel II. The monument holds Italy's Tomb of the Unknown Soldier of World War I. The Piazza Venezia is modern by Rome's standards—a mere eighty years old.

Old Roman villas, huge estates once owned by fabulously wealthy families, are now open to the public. The lawns have been turned into parks and the houses into museums. The Villa Borghese has a lawn as broad and heavily wooded as an endless forest, though the villa is within the city limits of Rome. The Villa Sciarra is famous for its fountains and its collection of rare plants. Once owned by the Medici family of Florence, it is today, very appropriately, a museum of fine arts.

The most magnificent of all the churches in Rome can be found in Vatican City, which can be described as a state within a city. With a population of a thousand and an area of about a sixth of a square mile (half a square kilometer), it is the smallest independent state in the world. Worldwide headquarters of the Roman Catholic church, it is ruled by the pope. It is also the home of some of the most spectacular works of art to be seen anywhere in the world.

The Sistine Chapel, with ceilings and walls decorated by Michelangelo's frescoes, is part of the Vatican. The Vatican Museum holds a priceless art collection ranging from ancient Egyptian pottery to paintings by Raphael, Titian, and Leonardo da Vinci.

Towering above the center of Vatican City is the awesome Saint Peter's Church, the largest Christian church in the world. Inside is the tomb believed to contain the remains of Saint Peter, the first pope of the Roman Catholic church. It took 150 years to build this remarkable church. Two of its principal architects were Bramante and Michelangelo. Ironically, it stands on the site of Nero's ancient circus grounds, where Christians were executed by the hundreds.

In Rome, there is a car for every six people. The city's ancient

Rome's traffic jams are nightmares for drivers and pedestrians alike.

streets cannot tolerate such a crush, and traffic jams are
nightmarish. But there are no traffic problems deep underground
in the catacombs, a complex dug by the early Christians in the
third and fourth centuries. Situated on the outskirts of Rome, the
catacombs cover about 600 acres (243 hectares) of rooms and
winding corridors. The Christians used them to bury their dead,
and fine examples of early Christian art can be seen in wall
frescoes. During the time of Roman persecution, Christians took
refuge in the catacombs. After the Fall of Rome, they were
forgotten and weren't rediscovered until 1578. Today electric
lights illuminate the frescoes for visitors on tours. Guides caution
people to stay in line. Anyone who wanders off faces the very real
danger of becoming lost in the maze of corridors.

Rome's Ancient City holds thrills for history-minded visitors. A
climb up the Palatine Hill might cross the spot where Rome was
founded more than twenty-five hundred years ago. At the Roman
Forum one can stand on the site where the senate debated, where
Julius Caesar was killed, and where Romulus—one of the

Hundreds of cats live in the ruins of Rome's Colosseum.

legendary founders of Rome—is said to be buried. The crumbling walls of the ancient Colosseum still stand, forever echoing the sounds of clashing gladiators' swords and the cheers of bloodthristy spectators. Today the inside of the Colosseum swarms with hundreds of stray cats who live in a shambles of tumbledown bricks.

Many Roman structures in the Ancient City are remarkably well preserved. The Baths of Caracalla are especially impressive. In the late afternoons, Romans gathered at these baths to wash away the sweat and grime of the day. Best preserved of all the ruins is the Pantheon, completed in A.D. 126 to honor the Roman gods. Another landmark is Trajan's Column, erected to honor one of the "five good emperors." It is appropriate that this column should tower above its neighboring structures, because under Trajan the empire's borders reached their greatest expanse.

The Fountain of Trevi is one of the most famous tourist attractions in Rome.

Of Rome's many fountains, the largest and most famous is the *Fontana di Trevi.* An old legend says that if a visitor turns his back to the Trevi Fountain and tosses a coin over his right shoulder, into its basin, he will surely return to Rome someday. On any summer afternoon, dozens of tourists can be seen performing this ritual.

Anyone who has been to Italy longs to return. More than a hundred years ago, English poet Percy Bysshe Shelley expressed his yearning for Italy:

> How beautiful is sunset, when the glow
> Of Heaven descends upon a land like thee,
> Thou Paradise of Exiles, Italy!

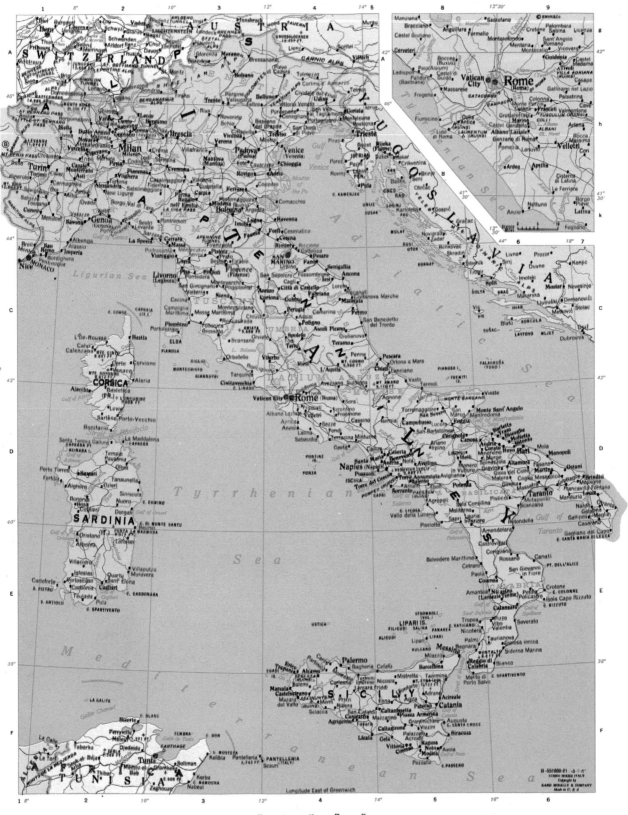

MINI-FACTS AT A GLANCE

GENERAL INFORMATION

Official Name: Republic of Italy *(Repubblica Italiana)*

Capital: Rome

Official Language: Italian

Other Languages: German is spoken in the Alto Adige region on the Austrian border, and in the Calabria and Basilicata regions of eastern Italy there is an Albanian-speaking minority. French and Serbo-Croatian are heard in areas bordering France and Yugoslavia.

Government: Italy is a republic. The constitution, written in 1948, calls for a parliament with two houses elected for five years. The senate has 315 elected members representing various regions, and 7 life senators. The chamber of deputies has 630 members. The president of the republic, elected by parliament for seven years, is the official head of state. The council of ministers is comparable to an executive branch of government. The president of the republic appoints the president of the council, or premier. On the recommendations of the premier, he also appoints other ministers who head various government departments. The council is responsible to parliament. The country is divided into twenty regions. Each region has a regional council elected every five years. The council is a legislature. The *giunta regionale* holds executive power and is responsible to the regional council.

Flag: The national flag of Italy is a rectangle with three vertical sections of red, white, and green. The green is next to the pole, the white in the middle, and the red on the outer side. Because of its three colors, the flag is called the *Tricolore*.

National Song: The music of the Italian national anthem was composed in 1847 by Michele Novaro, and set to the words of a poem by Goffredo Mameli, who was a young soldier serving with Garibaldi's Red Shirts. The song, known as "L'Inno di Mameli," has been the official anthem since 1946.

Religion: 95 percent of the Italian people are Roman Catholic.

Money: The Italian lira is the official monetary unit. It is equal to 100 centesimi. The plural of lira is lire. The average exchange rate of lire to dollars in early 1984 was about 1,600 lire per dollar.

Weights and Measures: The metric system is used.

Population: 57,140,355 (estimated population, January 1, 1981)

Cities:

Rome	2,916,414
Milan	1,655,599
Naples	1,219,362
Turin	1,143,263
Genoa	774,643
Palermo	698,254
Bologna	466,593
Florence	460,924
Catania	398,168
Bari	387,710
Venice	352,453

(Population figures as of January 1, 1981)

GEOGRAPHY

Land Regions: Italy's eight land regions include the Alpine Slope, the Po Valley, the Adriatic Plain, the Apennines, Apulia and the Southeastern Plains, the Western Uplands and Plains, and two large islands: Sicily and Sardinia.

Borders: Countries that border Italy are France on the northwest, Switzerland and Austria on the north, and Yugoslavia on the northeast. Italy is also ringed by several seas: the Ligurian and the Tyrrhenian on the west, the Ionian and the Mediterranean on the south, and the Adriatic on the east.

Highest Point: Monte Bianco (Mont Blanc), 15,771 ft. (4,807 m)

Lowest Point: Sea level

Rivers: The longest river in Italy is the Po; it flows for 400 mi. (643.7 km) across the top of the Italian boot. The Tiber flows through Rome and the Arno flows through Florence.

Coastline: 2,685 mi. (4,321 km)

Lakes: Most of Italy's largest and best-known lakes lie in the Lake District at the foot of the Alps in the far north of the country. These lakes include Maggiore, Orta, Lugano (with Switzerland), Como, Iseo, and Garda. The latter is Italy's largest lake. It is 32 mi. (51.5 km) long and up to 11 mi. (17.7 km) wide.

Mountains: Italy is largely mountainous. Thirty-five percent of the land is made up of mountains more than 2,300 ft. (701 m) high, 42 percent is hills, and only 23 percent consists of plains.

The former fishing village of Portofino on the Ligurian Sea

Climate: Italy's climate is extremely varied. Supposedly, more snow falls in the Italian Alps than in Iceland. North-central Tuscany can be wet and chilly, but Sicily is almost tropical. Rome can be stifling in midsummer, but by early afternoon the city is usually cooled by the *ponentino*, a fresh breeze from the sea. In Turin, the difference between the average summer and winter temperature is great. In the winter, the average is 32.5°F. (0.3°C) and in summer it is 74°F. (23°C). In the Apennines, the severity of winter varies according to the altitude. The annual mean temperature at Urbino is 53.8°F. (12.1°C) and at Potenza it is 54.5°F. (12.5°C). In Reggio di Calabria, in the south, the annual mean temperature is 64.7°F. (18.2°C). In Sicily, farther south, the annual mean temperature at Palermo is 64.4°F. (18.0°C).

Greatest Distances: North to south—708 mi. (1,139 km)
East to west—130 mi. (209 km)

Area: 116,000 sq. mi. (301,000 km²)

NATURE

Trees: Around the Lombardy lakes, evergreen, cork oak, European olive, cypress, and cherry laurel. At higher elevations, in Alpine regions, beech, deciduous larch, and Norway spruce. In the Po Valley, there are poplars and Scotch pine. In the Apennine region, holm oak, olive, carob, and Aleppo pine. In the Mediterranean area, cork oak, Aleppo pine, truffle oak, chestnut, flowering ash, and Oriental plane.

Fish, ocean: Red mullet, dentex, white man-eater shark, bluefin tuna, swordfish

Fish, freshwater: Brown trout, sturgeon, eel

Animals: Many animals have died off because of abuse by humans. Some of those still in existence are marmots, ermines, and Alpine rabbits, among the smaller animals. Larger animals include the ibex, chamois, roe, fox, and wolf.

Birds: Black grouse, golden eagle, capercaillie (wood grouse), mountain partridge

EVERYDAY LIFE:

Food: Italians pride themselves on their wonderful cooking. Dishes are specific not only to a region, but to particular cities. Naples, for example, is best known for plain pizza pie and stuffed peppers. In Genoa there are *gnocchi al pesto* (tiny dumplings with basil and garlic sauce) and *trenette* (a kind of long, narrow noodle). Some dishes are prepared only seasonally, such as the Roman *abbacchio al formo* (baked spring lamb). Italians are famous for their pastas, which come in many sizes, shapes, and colors, and their sauces, which come in many varieties. Wine is very important to an Italian meal. Until recently, Italian wines were noted only for their quantity, rather than their quality. But that is changing.

Housing: The constitution encourages home ownership. Until recently, however, most families were unable to own their own homes, and many lived in crowded apartments. The 1971 census, for example, revealed that there were more than 15 million homes of various sorts with an average of one person per room.

Holidays:
New Year's Day (January 1)
Epiphany (January 6)
Easter Monday
Feast of St. Joseph (March 19)
Liberation Day (April 25)
Labor Day (May 1)
National Day (June 2)
Assumption (August 15)
All Saints' Day (November 1)
Armistice Day (November 4)
Immaculate Conception (December 8)
Christmas Day (December 25)
Feast of St. Stephen (December 26)

Culture: Italian culture is very old and respected throughout the world. There are world-renowned figures in the visual arts, music, theater, dance, literature, and crafts. Important names in Italian art and architecture throughout the ages include Giotto, Donatello, Brunelleschi, Michelangelo, Leonardo da Vinci, and Bernini. In modern times there have been Modigliani, Umberto Boccioni, and Giacomo Balla.

Italian opera has led the world in this art form. The birth of opera took place in 1600 with the first performance of *Euridice*. But it came to full flower in the nineteenth century with composers such as Rossini, Verdi, Bellini, and Donizetti, whose operas are performed regularly throughout the world.

In literature, works by Dante, Petrarch, and Boccaccio have remained classics. In Dante's *The Divine Comedy*, the author takes a moving journey from Hell to Purgatory to Paradise. Petrarch is known as a love poet; Boccaccio gives his readers a fascinating inside view of Italian society in the 1300s. In the twentieth century, such writers as Alberto Moravia, Italo Calvino, Ignazio Silone, and Natalia Ginzburg have made their marks as novelists.

Filmmaking is the newest artistic explosion to hit Italy. Movies such as Vittorio De Sica's *The Bicycle Thief* and Roberto Rossellini's *Open City* have become classic statements on Italian postwar life. More recently, Federico Fellini and Lina Wertmuller, with their bizarre fantasies of Italian life, have become popular.

Language: Italian is a Romance language, meaning that it is a modern and regionalized variation on the old spoken Latin. Other Romance languages include French, Spanish, Portuguese, and Rumanian. Latin has influenced other languages as well, including English, which contains many words with Latin roots.

Sports and Recreation: Italians love spectator sports, particularly soccer, and they love to bet on the games. Bicycle racing and auto and motorcycle racing also have very big followings.

Schools: Education is compulsory and free for children between the ages of six and fourteen. At that time, a student who decides to stay in school begins a five-year program at a *liceo*. Those who pass the final *liceo* exam may go on to college.

Health: A national health service subsidizes medical care for everyone. Minimum charges are made for medical examinations and hospital treatment. All workers are eligible for benefits under a national medical insurance program.

ECONOMY AND INDUSTRY

Principal Products:
Agriculture: Almonds, cheese, figs, grapes, olives, lemons, peaches, apples, wheat, barley, potatoes, sugar beets, tobacco, tomatoes
Manufacturing: Automobiles, carved ivory and marble, sewing machines, typewriters, designer clothes, glasswork, ceramics, jewelry, shipbuilding, chemicals
Mining: Asbestos, bauxite, marble, mercury, sulfur, zinc

Communication: Most of Italy's daily newspapers appear in the north. The total daily circulation in 1981 was approximately 5 million. There are about 430 nondaily newspapers and over 4,000 periodicals published in Italy. Italian newspapers often struggle financially and must depend on a large corporation or a political party for support. There are more than 1,000 publishing houses in Italy.

The state once had a monopoly on broadcasting in Italy. But since 1974, there has been some relaxation of restrictions. A law passed in 1975 guarantees the objectivity of newscasts, and the two government stations are now being challenged by hundreds of private commercial stations. A dozen or so television stations are now available in most parts of Italy.

Transportation: The Italian railroads are administered by an agency controlled by the Minister of Transport. Most Italian railroads are owned by the state. The first railroad, between Naples and Portici, began operation in 1839. There are 12,500 mi. (20,117 km) of state-run railways, of which 5,396 mi. (8,684 km) are electrified. There are twenty-seven other local and municipal railway companies.

There are about 197,000 mi. (317,044 km) of roads in Italy, including about 25,000 mi. (40,234 km) of national highways.

Italy is served by *Alitalia* and three other domestic airlines—*ATI, Itavia,* and *Alisard.* There are six major seaports and thirty-five smaller ports, which handle millions of tons of goods each year. There are more than 1,500 mi. (2,414 km) of inland waterways made up of rivers, lakes, and canals.

IMPORTANT DATES

753 B.C.—Traditional date of the founding of Rome by Romulus

264-146 B.C.—Punic Wars

58-51 B.C.—Caesar conquers Gaul and invades Britain

44 B.C.—Caesar assassinated

27 B.C.—Augustus becomes first emperor of Rome

A.D. 313—Emperor Constantine officially recognizes Christianity

376-476—Invasions by Visigoths, Ostrogoths, Vandals, and Huns

476—Rome sacked; end of Western Roman Empire; Teutonic chief Odoacer becomes emperor

568—Lombards attack Rome

800—Pope Leo III crowns the Frankish King Charlemagne as Holy Roman Emperor

11th to 14th centuries—Power struggle between popes and emperors; rise of merchant states such as Genoa and Venice; rise of city-states such as Florence, Milan, and Siena

1016-1091—Normans settle in southern Italy

1220-1250—Swabian monarch Frederick II rules the south as Holy Roman Emperor

1453—Fall of Constantinople to Islam, marking the end of the Eastern Empire

1527—Spanish sack Rome

1494-1559—Italy becomes a battleground on which France and Spain struggle for power

1701-1748—Wars of Spanish and Austrian Succession: foreign powers fight over Italian territory

1796—Napoleon invades Italy

1815—Congress of Vienna; Napoleon overthrown

1815-1861—Risorgimento movement gathers strength

1860—Garibaldi and followers march on Sicily, then move to mainland, capturing Naples

1861—First national parliament formed under leadership of Count Cavour; Victor Emmanuel II proclaimed king; Cavour dies

1866—Nationalists capture Venetia

1870—Unification of Italy completed; pope loses civil powers

1870-1915—Consolidation of Italian kingdom; some colonial expansion

1915-1918—Italy joins Allies in World War I

1922—Fascists march on Rome; Mussolini becomes dictator

1936—Mussolini conquers Ethiopia

1940—Italy joins Germany in World War II

1943—Italy loses African possessions; Italian cities bombed by Allies; American troops invade Sicily; King Victor Emmanuel III deposes Mussolini; Italy surrenders to Allies; Germans invade northern Italy

1945—End of World War II; Mussolini captured and killed by anti-Fascists

1946—Italian republic is formed

1949—Italy joins NATO

1955—Italy joins the United Nations

1976—Aldo Moro's coalition government of Christian Democrats and Republicans resigns

1977—Communists allowed a policy-making role in government

1978—Minority government of Giulio Andreotti forced to resign; former Premier Aldo Moro kidnapped and murdered; President Giovanni Leone resigns as a result of allegations of corruption; Alessandro Pertini becomes first Socialist president of the republic

1979—The second Andreotti administration collapses; Francesco Cossiga forms minority "government of truce"

1980—Earthquake in southern Italy kills thousands

1981—Government of Arnaldo Forlani resigns as a result of the "P-2 affair," the worst scandal in recent Italian history; Giovanni Spadolini forms a majority coalition government, becoming the first non-Christian Democrat premier since the start of the republic

1982—Forty-second government since 1948 is in power

IMPORTANT PEOPLE

Leon Battista Alberti (1404-1472), Renaissance architect, scholar, painter, author

Giulio Andreotti (1919-   ), former premier

Michelangelo Antonioni (1912-   ), film director

Giovanni Lorenzo Bernini (1598-1680), sculptor, architect, and painter

Giovanni Boccaccio (1313-1375), writer, considered to be one of the founders of the Renaissance

Filippo Brunelleschi (1377-1446), architect, designed the Pitti Palace and the dome of the Cathedral of Santa Maria del Fiore in Florence

Alberto Burri, (1915-   ), painter

Gaius Julius Caesar (100-44 B.C.), military leader, statesman, and writer

Enrico Caruso (1873-1921), operatic tenor

Gaius Cassius Longinus (d. 42 B.C.), Roman general and conspirator against Caesar

Camillo Benso di Cavour (1810-1861), first premier of united Italy

Charlemagne (724-814), first Holy Roman Emperor, 800-814

Christopher Columbus (1451-1506), explorer, discovered the American continent while trying to reach Asia

Marcus Licinius Crassus (115?-53 B.C.), Roman politician

Dante Alighieri (1265-1321), poet, author of *The Divine Comedy*

Alcide De Gasperi (1881-1954), premier, 1945-1953

Grazia Deledda (1871-1936), Nobel Prize-winning writer

Vittorio De Sica (1901-1974), film director

Gaetano Donizetti (1797-1848), composer of operas, including *Don Pasquale*

Federico Fellini (1920-   ), movie director

Alessandro di Mariano Filipepi (Sandro Botticelli), (1445-1510), painter

Arnaldo Forlani (1925-   ), former premier

Frederick II (1194-1250), Holy Roman Emperor 1212-50; soldier, scientist, poet; a forerunner of the Renaissance

Galileo (1564-1642), astronomer and physicist

Giotto di Bondone (1267?-1337), first major artist to experiment with perspective; major influence on Renaissance painters who followed him

Giuseppe Garibaldi (1807-1882), leader in the movement for the unification of Italy

Humbert I (1844-1900), king of Italy

Humbert II (1904-   ), king of Italy

Julius II (1443-1513), pope who commissioned rebuilding of St. Peter's Church and painting of Sistine Chapel

Justinian (I) the Great (483-565), Byzantine emperor, 527-565

Leo III (750?-816), pope who crowned Charlemagne as Holy Roman Emperor

Giovanni Leone (1908-   ), president of the republic

Giacomo Leopardi (1798-1837), poet

Leopold of Tuscany (1747-1792), duke and political reformer

Marcus Aemilius Lepidus (d. 13 B.C.), part of Roman triumvirate

Carlo Levi (1902-1975), painter; author, wrote *Christ Stopped at Eboli*

Titus Livius (Livy) (59 B.C.-A.D. 17), Roman historian

Niccolo Machiavelli (1469-1527), statesman and political philosopher

Luigi Maggi (1867-1946), film pioneer

Alessandro Manzoni (1785-1873), romantic poet, playwright and novelist

Marcus Antonius (Mark Antony) (83?-30 B.C.), Roman orator, general, and part of a triumvirate

Masaccio (Tommaso di Giovanni di Simone Guidi) (1401-1428), painter, developed principles of perspective further than Giotto had done

Giuseppe Mazzini (1805-1872), leader in the cause of Italian independence and unification

Lorenzo de' Medici (1449-1492), Florentine statesman, ruler, patron of the arts

Michelangelo Buonarroti (1475-1564), sculptor, painter, architect, and poet

Maria Montessori (1870-1952), physician and pioneer in progressive education

Alberto Moravia (1907-   ), writer and journalist

Aldo Moro (1916-1978), premier who was kidnapped and murdered

Benito Mussolini (1883-1945), Fascist dictator

Napoleon Bonaparte (1769-1821), first French emperor after the French Revolution, conqueror of Italy

Chief Odoacer (434?-493), first barbarian ruler of Italy

Niccoló Paganini (1782-1840), composer and violinist

Giovanni Pierluigi da Palestrina (1525-1594), composer

Alessandro Pertini (1896-   ), first socialist president of the republic

Francesco Petrarca (Petrarch) (1304-1374), pre-Renaissance poet

Luigi Pirandello (1867-1936), dramatist and novelist

Marco Polo (1254-1324), Venetian traveler and trader; spent seventeen years in the service of Kublai Khan in China

Gnaeus Pompeius Magnus (Pompey the Great) (104-48 B.C.), Roman general and statesman

Giacomo Puccini (1858-1924), composer of operas, including *La Boheme, Tosca,* and *Madame Butterfly*

Remus and Romulus, legendary founders of Rome

Ottorino Respighi (1879-1936), composer

Roberto Rossellini (1906-1977), postwar film director

Gioacchino Rossini (1792-1868), composer of operas, including *The Barber of Seville*

Giuseppe Santomaso (1907-   ), painter

Raffaello Sanzio (Raphael), (1483-1520), painter

Ignazio Silone (1900-1978), novelist and political activist

Giovanni Spadolini (1925-   ), first non-Christian Democrat premier

Spartacus (d. 71 B.C.), Roman slave and leader of revolt

Stephen II (d. 757), pope who asked the Franks for help against the Lombards

Italo Svevo (1861-1928), writer

Torquato Tasso (1544-1595), late Renaissance poet

Giuseppe Verdi (1813-1901), composer of operas, including *Rigoletto, Aida,* and *La Traviata*

Victor Emmanuel II (1820-1878), king of Sardinia and first king of Italy

Victor Emmanuel III (1869-1947), last king of Italy

Leonardo da Vinci (1452-1519), Florentine painter, sculptor, architect, and engineer

Luchino Visconti (1906-1976), film director

Antonio Vivaldi (1678-1741), composer

ROMAN EMPERORS

Augustus (Octavian)	27 B.C.-A.D. 14	Carinus	283-285
Tiberius	14-37	and Numerian	283-284
Caligula	37-41	Diocletian	284-305
Claudius	41-54	and Maximian	286-305
Nero	54-68	Constantius I	305-306
Galba	68-69	Galerius	305-311
Otho	69	Maxentius	306-312
Vitellius	69	Constantine I (the Great)	306-337
Vespasian	69-70	Licinius	308-324
Titus	79-81	Constanius II	337-361
Domitian	81-96	Constantine II	337-340
Nerva	96-98	Constans	337-350
Trajan	98-117	Julian	361-363
Hadrian	117-138	Jovian	363-364
Antoninus Pius	138-161	Valentinian I	364-375
Marcus Aurelius Antoninus	161-180	Valens	364-378
Commodus	180-192	Gratian	375-383
Pertinax	193	Valentinian II	375-392
Didius Julianus	193	Eugenius	392-394
Septimius Severus	193-211	Theodosius I	379-395
Caracalla	211-217		
Macrinus	217-218		
Elagabalus	218-222	**Western Empire**	
Alexander Severus	222-235	Honorius	395-423
Maximus Thrax	235-238	John	424
Gordianus I	238	Valentinian III	425-455
Gordianus II	238	Petronius Maximus	455
Pupienus and Balbinus	238	Avitus	455-456
Gordianus III	238-244	Majorian	457-461
Philip the Arabian	244-249	Libius Severus	461-465
Decius	249-251	Recimir	465-467
Gallus	251-253	Anthemius	467-472
Aemilianus	253	Olybrius	472-473
Valerian	253-260	Glycerius	473
Gallienus	253-268	Julius Nepos	473-475
Claudius II	268-270	Romulus Augustulus	475-476
Aurelian	270-275		
Tacitus	275-276		
Florian	276		
Probus	276-282		
Carus	282-283		

INDEX

Page numbers that appear in boldface type indicate illustrations

About the Author

R. Conrad Stein was born and grew up in Chicago. He enlisted in the Marine Corps at the age of eighteen and served for three years. He then attended the University of Illinois where he received a Bachelor's degree in history. He later studied in Mexico, earning an advanced degree from the University of Guanajuato. Mr. Stein is the author of many other books, articles, and short stories written for young people.

Mr. Stein is married to Deborah Kent, who is also a writer of books for young readers. They have a daughter, Janna.